CW00552400

Inside the Park

Points of Interest

Historical Site

Buildings in the Park

Rouken Glen Park

heritage lottery fund

LOTTERY FUNDED

East Renfrewshire COUNCIL

Discovering
Rouken Glen Park

First published in Great Britain in 2016 by

East Renfrewshire Council
Environment Department
Thornliebank Office
190 Carnwadric Road
Glasgow G46 8HR

©East Renfrewshire Council 2016

Printed in the United Kingdom by J Thomson Colour Printers

Acknowledgements

With many thanks to the Heritage Lottery Fund,
Glasgow Life and the Mitchell Library, Archaeology Scotland,
the Geological Society of Glasgow, Mairi Sutherland and
Rouken Glen Park staff.

Special thanks to the volunteers who compiled this book:
Andrew Eadie, Harry Rutherford, Suzanne Ewins, Lorraine
Dunn, Andy Melvin, Oliver Fielden and Rae Condie.
Additional thanks go to Stuart Nisbet for his contribution.
Edited by Stuart Nisbet and Sharon McMurtrie.

First published in November 2016

ISBN: 978-1-871215-08-3

Design www.traffic-design.co.uk

Cover - *The Waterfall from
The Devil's Staircase c2015
Map Flag 01, 14*

Opposite - *The Boating Pond c2015
Map Flag 02*

Foreword
Councillor Vincent Waters

As Convenor for Environment it has been my great
pleasure to be involved in the Rouken Glen Park project.

Above - *Councillor Vincent Waters
in Rouken Glen Park*
Opposite - *The Glen Walk*

With the support of the Heritage Lottery Fund and
East Renfrewshire Council, the park has been transformed
over the last four years to a point where it is confirmed
as one of Scotland's top outdoor visitor attractions.

Not only has the park benefitted from substantial investment
in its physical fabric, but through the endeavours of local
volunteers, a comprehensive history of the park has now
been brought together for the first time. Whilst for many
the play area, boating pond and walks through the Glen
are reason enough to visit Rouken Glen, the discoveries,
recollections and historical images contained in this book
will act as a further reason to explore the park.

I would like to thank the volunteers and council staff for
all their efforts to gather and piece together the story of
Rouken Glen Park and I hope that you will enjoy reading
this book as much as I have.

Councillor Vincent Waters
October 2016

The discoveries, recollections and historical images contained in this book will act as a further reason to explore the park.

Contents

20th Century
in the Park

21st Century
in the Park

Geology
of the park

The park dates back to Prehistoric times, it has a rich geological history which has been attracting people for hundreds of years. Examples of the park's history are still visible today.

Discover the parks geology

Layers or beds of rock - sand, silt, mud, and coal along the banks of the Auldhouse Burn
Map Flag 13

Site of Special Scientific Interest

The rocks in Rouken Glen were mostly formed during the Carboniferous geological period about 325 million years ago. At this time Scotland was close to the equator with a humid tropical climate. The area was part of a huge coastal plain on the edge of a shallow sea – a bit like parts of Borneo today.

Sometimes the sea flooded the land and the shallow tropical seas allowed corals to grow and marine plants and animals to thrive. Sometimes there were large river deltas and muddy swamps. The thick sandstones represent river channels. The thin-bedded sandstone layers formed in wet swamps, or in the shallow tidal seas. Coals represent forests growing in drier swamps and mudstone represents quiet water – either in swamps or offshore. Limestones represent deeper marine conditions. The Rouken Glen gorge is the best remaining place in Scotland to see these rocks.

In the Auldhouse Burn there are a very important series of rock layers – the Orchard Beds, exposed in and around the burn. When geologists talk about rock beds they are referring to the smallest divisions they can identify in sedimentary rock layers. Each bed demonstrates a distinct set of environmental conditions present at the time the sediments were deposited. These are called the Orchard Beds because they were first found in the Orchard Farm area of Thornliebank and Giffnock, where quarries were worked in the 19th Century.

These rocks provide a detailed record of changing environments and life in the sea 325 million years ago. The rocks contain lots of different kinds of fossils that provide evidence of marine creatures which lived in the sea or on the sea floor. The fossils were formed because the bodies of small dead creatures were quickly covered by underwater sediments like sand, silt and mud. As the layers of sediment built up they compacted into rocks surrounding the hard remains of the original creatures.

On the gorge above the Auldhouse Burn is a top thick layer of sandstone called Giffnock Sandstone. This rock was one of the most important building stones in the Glasgow area during the 19th century with quarries near Orchard Park Road, and at Braidbar, both in Giffnock, north east of Rouken Glen Park. The quarries are now mostly filled in so Rouken Glen is the best place to see the Giffnock Sandstone. Many of the houses in the area are built of this stone as well as some buildings in Glasgow city centre.

Rouken Glen Park's Orchard Beds Geo-trail can be downloaded from the Rouken Glen Park website **www.roukenglenpark.co.uk**

Top Left - *The Orchard Beds in the Auldhouse Burn*

Top Right - *Layers or beds of rock - sand, silt, mud, and coal*

Middle Right - *Layer of Giffnock Sandstone overhanging the Auldhouse Burn in The Glen*
Map Flag 13

Bottom Left - *Fossilised tree in the Meadow*
Map Flag 11

Bottom Middle - *Conglomerate in the park near the railway line*

Bottom Right - *Some of the fossils found in Rouken Glen shown next to a one pence coin to indicate size*

Archaeological Features Map

20th Century   19th Century   17th-18thCentury   Medieval   Prehistoric

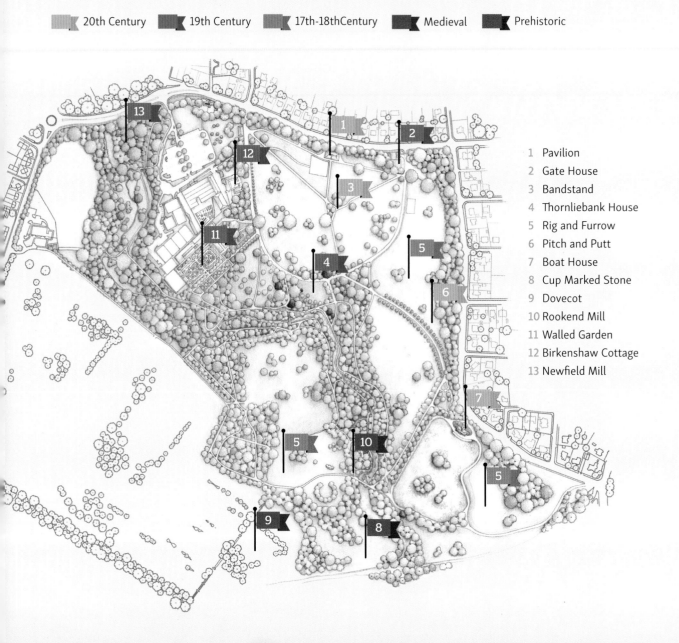

1 Pavilion
2 Gate House
3 Bandstand
4 Thornliebank House
5 Rig and Furrow
6 Pitch and Putt
7 Boat House
8 Cup Marked Stone
9 Dovecot
10 Rookend Mill
11 Walled Garden
12 Birkenshaw Cottage
13 Newfield Mill

Marking the Land: The Park in Prehistory

The Bulletin. Wednesday, November 10, 1957.

WHERE DRUIDS STAR-GAZED

These "cup and ring" markings have been discovered at Cathcart Castle golf course, near Glasgow. While excavations were being made during the construction of a new green workmen came upon a large slab of rock carved with the ancient Druidical symbols. Above is seen the largest of the rings.

For thousands of years people have been visiting the area known today as Rouken Glen.

Traces of their presence can be seen in ancient artwork painstakingly pecked into the bedrock with stone tools. Other more prominent cup and ring markings have been found close to the park in Cathcart Castle golf course. The park's cup-marked rock lies at the southwest end of the park beside the Glasgow to Neilston railway line. Cup and ring marks are believed to have been created sometime between the Late Neolithic and the Bronze Age (between 2000 and 750BC). This was a time of transition for the people living in the area, when they first experimented with metal tools. Cup marks are found across Scotland, but rarely by themselves, like the Rouken Glen example. Thus it was hoped the weathered bedrock had more secrets to reveal about the park's landscape.

Left - Cup and ring marks on Cathcart Golf Course, south east of Rouken Glen (Bulletin 10 November 1957)

Archaeology in the Park

The cup marks were examined as one of Archaeology Scotland's series of investigative community projects in the park, between 2013 and 2015.

Analysis was carried out using a technique called Reflectance Transformation Imaging (RTI). This uses photography to record shadows produced by a single light source moving around a static point (like a torch moving around a tennis ball). For best effect, it is done in darkness or low light conditions, so during the day a tarpaulin was used to block out the light. A computer programme then used Photogrammetry (multiple photographs knitted together to craft a single 3D image) to reveal marks invisible to the naked eye. After the use of RTI, it was clear that the stone's surface originally had at least three or four distinct cup marks, one possibly with an associated ring, as well as other peck-marked designs.

Right - Setting up the RTI equipment at Rouken Glen's cup marked stone

The Beginning of
The Historical Period

Top - *Excavations at Rookend Mill*
Middle Left - *The remains of Rookend Mill, Summer 2015*
Middle Right - *Rookend Millstone*
Bottom - *Archway revealed*
Map Flag 28

Opposite Left - *Rookend Mill from John Ainslie's plan of 1789*
Opposite Right - *Artist's impression of how Rookend Mill may have looked when in use c1700 Drawing courtesy of Archaeology Scotland*

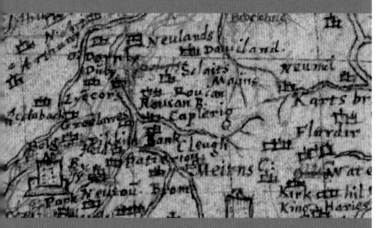

Origin of the Name 'Rouken Glen'

The name of the park comes from a portion of land within the modern park, known by various spellings, including Roucan, Rokand, Rockend and Rouken. The name is mentioned in The Eglinton Charters (papers of the Earl of Eglinton family) from the 1580s. It also appears on the earliest detailed map of the area, surveyed by Timothy Pont in the 1590s. The name 'Roucan' seems to have come from Old Norse, which was used to name various places in East Renfrewshire from the 10th Century.

Above - *Timothy Pont Map 1590s indicating properties in East Renfrewshire*

Highlights of Rouken Glen Park

Rookend Mill, Auldhouse Burn and The Waterfall

Rookend Mill

John Ainslie's plan of 1789 depicts several structures on an old mill, one of which is Rookend Mill. Today the ruins of the mill lie hidden in vegetation on the steep side of the Glen.

The mill was powered by a lade cut along the slope, from the original crest of Rouken Falls. Later, about 200 years ago, the falls were doubled in height by the large dam behind the falls.

Archaeology Scotland set out to investigate Rookend Mill in 2014. Working alongside volunteers, vegetation which surrounds the mill was cleared and a trench opened inside the building. This revealed a stone arch, through which water may have entered the mill.

Clearing of the site also uncovered a broken mill stone, a slot in the outer wall possibly for a wheel axle, and part of a stone-built channel. Further back, on the falls, the channel was cut into the bedrock of the burn, and still flows with water after heavy rain.

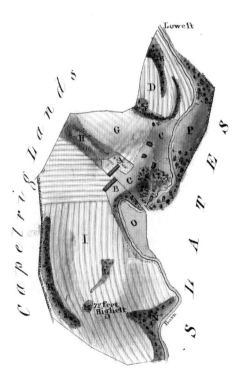

The Waterfall

Opposite - *Top of the waterfall, Autumn 2015.*
Map Flag 01

Top - *Foot of the waterfall c1910*

Middle - *Top of the waterfall c.1912.*

Bottom - *Foot of the waterfall 2015*

The Auldhouse Burn

The Doocot

The Auldhouse burn flows from the Brother Loch, a largely man-made reservoir on the Mearns Moor, approximately 5 miles south of Rouken Glen Park, all the way down to where it meets the White Cart Water at Pollokshaws, approximately 3 miles north of the park. The burn has various names along its length. South of the park it is called the Capelrig Burn until joined by the Broom Burn. North of the park it is sometimes called the Shaws Burn.

The burn enters the park through a bridge under the railway from Glasgow to Neilston.

Initially the burn fills the reservoir behind the dam at Rouken falls. After passing over the dramatic falls into the rocky gorge, it follows the Glen. It flows down behind the site of the Rouken Glen Mansion House, to the former reservoirs for Newfield textile works. The burn exits the modern park through a culvert under Rouken Glen Road. Until the 1980s, an additional triangle of land north of Rouken Glen Road was also part of the park. The burn exits the park under Spiersbridge Road into a reservoir for Thornliebank Works.

Apart from providing the name for the park, industrial use of the burn also originates with the mill at Rouken (Rokandmyll).

The earliest upstanding building in the area is the late medieval Doocot (or Dovecot) on Deaconsbank Golf Course, bounding the park.

As the name suggests, the building was once home to pigeons. The young birds, or squabs, became tasty dishes for the wealthy owners of the doocot. This once-impressive structure was abandoned and left to deteriorate for many years, but has now been restored through the HLF park improvement project.

This site was recorded by photography during another Archaeology Scotland training session, with one volunteer producing a black and white rendition of the structure.

During the work, it was clear that Deaconsbank Doocot had been modified over time, with a large window, which is now blocked up. It is also likely that the doocot would have originally been covered in lime based harling, and the white lime washed building would have stood out in the landscape.

Left - *Auldhouse Burn leaving the park at culvert under Rouken Glen Road at the north of the park*
Map Flag 13

Right - *Drawing of how the Doocot may have originally looked, courtesy of Archaeology Scotland*
Map Flag 25

Devil's Staircase

The rock-cut stair, which climbs up beside the falls, is known as the Devil's Staircase. The name derives from a small devilish face with horns, which is carved (unknown date) at the side of the steps, at the midway point. There is a tradition that the face was carved by the masons who cut the steps out of the solid bedrock, in frustration at their difficult task of creating nearly 100 steps.

Left - The staircase devil
***Below**- The Devil's Staircase 2015*
Map Flag 14

Farming and Industry
in the park

The park hasn't always been a park for the people, it also has a very rich agricultural history.

Discover farming and industry in the park

*The top of the Dam
at Rouken Falls
Map Flag 01*

Highlights of Rouken Glen Park
The Farms Making up the Modern Park

The lands making up Rouken Glen Park were originally part of the Barony of Eastwood. The western border of the Barony was formed by the Auldhouse Burn.

1789

Left - The first large-scale plan of the park area is John Ainslie's Survey of 1789

Right - Sketch plan of The Barony of Eastwood Based on John Ainslie's Survey, Edinburgh, 1789

Most of Eastwood traditionally belonged to the Earls of Eglinton. Small portions to the west of the burn, including Rouken and Deaconsbank Farms, were part of the estates of Capelrig and Nether Pollok. One of the earliest surviving written records for the park area dates from 1530. It is a deed by Hugh, first Earl of Eglington, giving his grandson, Hugh, Master of Eglington, possession of the lands of Corslie.

Corslie included Rokandmyll, Brokellis, Sclatis, Byrkinschaw, Gyffnock, Cleuch, Orchart, Ovirdauidland, Braidbar, Nethirdauidland. The first three, better known as Rouken, Brocklees and Slates were the farms which make up most of the park today.

John Ainslie's 1789 plan of part of the Barony of Eastwood. The current Rouken Glen Park boundary is highlighted in red.

The plan shows a rural landscape. The only obvious divisions of the land are between individual farms, such as Brocklees and Slates. Rookend farm, with its meal mill, is located in the southwest corner. Other strips to the west of the burn, parts of Capelrig and Pollok, are shown blank. The only buildings within what will become the park are at Brocklees (Newfield printfield and Brocklees farm steading, see below) and at Rouken mill. The hatching on the plan indicates arable and pasture land use. Apart from open farmland, areas of trees are growing down the Glen, along the Auldhouse Burn.

Early Farming - Rig and Furrow

In the 16th and 17th centuries, the area which became the park was a mixture of farmland and woodland. The majority of folk earned a living from the land. Arable land contained distinctive large banks and ditches known as 'rig and furrow'.

These dramatic corrugations on the landscape were formed over the years by ploughing, using a large plough pulled by a team of oxen (later by horses). Depictions of rig and furrow can be seen on William Roy's Map in the 1750s, and surviving fragments can still be seen in Rouken Glen Park's southeast corner, close to Whitecraigs station. These were recorded during a walkover survey with students from the University of Glasgow, the University of Strathclyde and dedicated local volunteers. The survey identified at least three separate groups of rig and furrow, travelling in different directions, suggesting three separate fields. The rig and furrow also runs under the woodland at this end of the park, showing that it predates the trees. A field boundary was also identified, running between two areas of rig and furrow. The boundary consisted of three large mature deciduous trees growing over traces of a much reduced stone and turf bank.

Today Rouken Glen is one of the last surviving green spaces in the area. However it did not switch directly from farmland into a park. From the 1770s, the Glen was gradually altered by industry. At the same time its farmland was turned into a country retreat. This growing change of land use in the area, for agricultural, industrial, and leisure use, was partly due to the decline of the great wood of Eastwood, which at one time had covered much of the area. In 1773 the "Last woods of Eastwood" were advertised in the Glasgow press. At the same time, the arable land was in the process of being improved and enclosed. However, the land barely had time to be turned into modern, enclosed farms, before it was divided up for industrial and leisure use (as a small country estate).

Left - Old field boundary

Middle - Rig and furrow above the pond

Right - Tree planting over rig and furrow along Davieland Road
Map Flag 29

The Burn and Falls in the Glen

Apart from its valuable farmland, the other main strength of the area that became the park is the Auldhouse Burn. The biggest man-made influences to the land started with the founding of textile works along the burn.

This occurred for two reasons: first, the pure water in the burn which was ideal for bleaching and printing and second, thanks to the burn's steep fall through the Glen, which was dammed and diverted to create a big fall to drive the large water wheels of cotton mills and other machinery.

From the 1730s the earliest bleachfields and printfields in Scotland had been established at the foot of the burn at Pollokshaws. From the 1770s, four main types of industry would appear inside the park area:

Bleachfields

Cloth (which had previously been woven by handloom weavers in the home) was wetted in canals, then laid out on the grass in the daylight, to bleach it white.

Printfields

With the invention of chlorine-based bleaching powder from the 1790s, bleaching of textiles moved indoors and was combined with dyeing and printing. By 1800 the Auldhouse Burn had more than a dozen bleachfields and printfields, including one inside what is now the park.

Cotton Mills

From the 1770s cotton spinning mills sprang up in the area, using water power to drive machinery for the preparing and spinning of cotton wool into yarn for weaving. The County of Renfrew was the leading cotton spinning area in Scotland, with more than half of the cotton mills in Scotland. Rouken Glen played a part in this, with a big water powered cotton spinning mill down in the Glen.

Power Weaving Mills

Until the 1790s, weaving was done by hand, in the home. Gradually power-driven machinery was invented which allowed the weaving of coarse cloth in mills. Rouken Glen latterly had a power weaving mill, down in the Glen beside the cotton mill. Like the cotton mill, its water wheel was powered by the fall of water in the burn.

Newfield Bleachfield and Cotton Mills

Following the establishment of a bleachfield on the farm of Thornliebank (just outside the park), another bleachfield was founded on Brocklees Farm in the north west corner of the present park, west of the current Garden Centre carpark. It was named Newfield (New [bleach] field). Later a cotton mill was built on the site of the bleachfield.

Newfield Archaeology

In 2015 Archaeology Scotland opened a series of test pits at Newfield, to try to locate the mill lade and any remains of the cotton mill. It was discovered that the ground level over the site had been significantly raised and remodelled when the buildings were demolished. However the start of the mill lade can be seen in a blocked-up sandstone arch above the waterfall at Newfield.

Left - *Newfield overflow and blocked-up arch for Newfield cotton mill lade 1988*
Map Flag 26

Right - *Newfield Mill, Ordnance Survey 1858*

Bottom - *The Glen Falls*

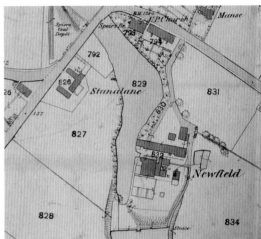

Highlights of Rouken Glen Park
Dams and Reservoirs in the Park

To operate on such a relatively small burn, the textile works had to build large dams to store up water, to spread out the supply during dry periods. Some of these dams, and their reservoirs and lades, survive in the Glen.

Newfield Dams

In 1789 the plan of Brocklees Farm shows not only the buildings at Newfield, but also its network of canals.

Around this time, a much larger dam, more than 5m high, was built to create a fall of water to drive the water wheel of Newfield cotton mill, which was built beside the bleachfield. The reservoir behind the big dam stretched right back along the Glen.

Over the years, the dams and buildings at Newfield were altered and expanded. Big changes were made to Newfield dam between the 1850s and 1890s. A water channel or 'lade' was built along the eastern side of the dam, and the reservoir was split into two, the current empty reservoir behind the dam, and the 'Duck Pond' which is now mostly silted up.

Top - Sketch of the Duck Pond, Newfield Reservoir and Dam, Newfield Mill and its lade

Left - Main sluice inlet to Newfield Reservoir from the Duck Pond

Right - Drained Dam at Rouken Falls 1983

Dam at Rouken Falls

By the 1820s another dam had been built on top of Rouken falls, to store more water. This curved masonry dam can be seen behind the bridge and doubled the height of the falls. This dam, and the reservoir behind it, was advertised from the 1820s for sale, and is shown on the 1858 Ordnance Survey map.

As mentioned, the main reservoir supplying Newfield (and for the various other textile works on the burn) was several miles further up the burn, at its source on Mearns Moor. There, a dam was built to enlarge the Brother Loch. From the 1790s this dam was jointly controlled by the owners of Newfield and the other printfields and cotton mills down at Thornliebank and Pollokshaws. Each morning, a worker had to ride up to the Brother Loch and raise the sluice, to release the water which powered all the works down the burn.

The buildings of the bleachfields, printfield and cotton mills may have come and gone, but the dams and their reservoirs remain in the park.

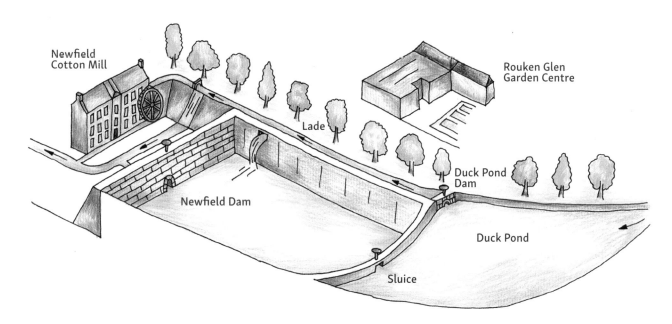

Newfield
Cotton Mill

Rouken Glen
Garden Centre

Lade

Duck Pond
Dam

Newfield Dam

Duck Pond

Sluice

The Osburns and Crums

Both Newfield bleachfield and cotton mill, (and also a similar bleachfield and cotton mill at Thornliebank downstream) were started in the 1770s by textile merchant Robert Osburn and his son William.

By 1789 part of the Osburns' business was facing bankruptcy. They advertised their cotton mill down at Thornliebank, plus their bleachfield which had by this time become a printfield. The advert included workers houses.

Following the death of Osburn's son William in 1791, Newfield and associated properties including the 'farm, dwelling houses, mill and other buildings, engines and bleaching items belonging to Mr Osburn' were advertised for sale. It continued in operation for a few years and a large water powered cotton mill was added, driven by a big dam in the park.

The works were gradually taken over by the Crum family. Initially the Crums acquired the Osburns' works at Thornliebank, then at Newfield. It is difficult to tell exactly when the transitions occurred, as the Crums did not own the works outright, but initially rented some of the buildings and lands. The Osburn family persisted as owners of parts of the works and lands into the 1820s.

Today the Osburns who founded Newfield and Thornliebank are almost forgotten, in favour of the later owners, the Crums. Newfield works inside the park is also forgotten, in favour of Thornliebank, which had more room for expansion and lasted longer. However, the Crums continued to be important in the park, not only with their works at Newfield, but by turning the parkland into a country estate.

1790 People in the Park

When textile works were established in a rural area, the owner had to build housing for the workforce. In the 1790s, the Osburns had already built some housing at Newfield, east of their works. By the 1830s Newfield works employed 200 people. Ten times this number were employed just downstream at Thornliebank. A new village began to develop, due to the work available in the textile works.

Opposite - *The Folly c2016*

Map Flag 17

The 19th Century
Preparation for a Park

1812 Estate

By 1812, much of Eastwood Parish was still owned by the Eglinton family whose main seat is near Irvine in Ayrshire (now Eglinton Country Park). The Eglinton's survey of the Barony of Eastwood by John Ainslie in 1789 includes sketches of the farm buildings. Some are shown without roofs, suggesting that the estate needed investment.

Further afield, the Eglintons were in financial trouble, due to spending large amounts of money attempting to construct a canal from Glasgow to Ardrossan via Paisley in 1806, which got no further than Johnstone.

On 13 August 1812, their Eastwood estate was sold by Hugh, 12th Earl of Eglinton, to John Anderson. By this time the individual farms were being subdivided for industry and water storage. John Anderson started selling off other parts from 1812, and his lands passed to his heir David Anderson Blair. By this time, parts of Slates and Thornliebank farms along the 'water of Ruken' were owned or rented by the Crum family.

1806 Rouken as a Country Estate

For much of the 19th century it was quite normal for industrialists to locate their homes inside their works. For several generations the Crums lived in a big house inside Thornliebank works.

This was partly to exercise control over their workforce. However once the family began to acquire water rights and land beside Rouken Glen, they also saw the opportunity to develop part of their land as a country retreat. Initially this was not for their own use, but to generate income from parts of their land which were becoming too small or fragmented to let as farms.

In 1806, exactly a century before the opening of Rouken Glen Park, the first signs appear of the lands being turned into leisure use. The Crums advertised fifteen acres of the 'lands of Rouken', as a situation for building a country villa. However they kept their options open, mixing residential use with further potential industrial use. The adverts included the burn, described as a 'considerable stream' running from Mearns Loch, with a fall of nearly 70 feet'. This was the total fall through the park, from Rouken Falls down to Newfield. The suggested use of the waterfall was as a paper mill. If this option had been taken up, and a big paper mill built at the waterfall, it is unlikely that the park would exist today. In the 1820s the remaining 70 acres of Brocklees unoccupied by industry were still let to farming tenants. The following decade, the portion of Brocklees to let as farmland had decreased to only 20 acres.

Left – *From RHP 3/170, vignette of Brocklees Farm*

1821 Newfield in Crisis

Like the Osburns earlier, by 1821 the Crums had fallen into deep financial trouble, with debts approaching £200,000. Their whole works at Newfield were put on the market.

The sale included 14 acres of the mill lands of Newfield, plus another 12 acres of adjacent arable land named Stonelaw Park, Mid Park and South Park. The exact location of these small pockets of land is unclear. The advert also included buildings and a fall of water of 18 feet (5.5m). By this time the cotton mill at Newfield had 4,000 spindles. A power weaving mill, also driven by water, had been added, with more than 80 power looms. Bleaching and printing was no longer carried out at Newfield, but had moved downstream to Thornliebank.

As in 1806, the lands of Rouken were also included in the potential sale (16 acres plus the waterfall) which were 'well known to afford one of the most romantic and beautiful situations for a villa'. By this time, the Crums were still renting much of their land and water rights. Newfield was rented from the Osburn family and rents were also paid for Brother Loch and Black Loch on Mearns Moor.

In addition to Newfield, the Crums were also forced to advertise their whole printing works, cotton mill and weaving factory at Thornliebank. This was also driven by the water stored in the Glen. Despite this financial hiccup, the Crums held onto their works and thrived for another 80 years.

The Crums

In 1783 John Crum was a grocer and cotton dealer in Glasgow, with a textile warehouse in the Gallowgate. It is likely that the Crum family initially rented pockets of Rouken Glen in the late 1790s when the Osburn family were trying to sell Newfield mill and its associated properties to pay their creditors.

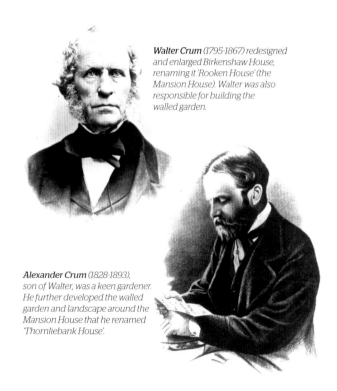

Walter Crum (1795-1867) redesigned and enlarged Birkenshaw House, renaming it 'Rooken House' (the Mansion House). Walter was also responsible for building the walled garden.

Alexander Crum (1828-1893), son of Walter, was a keen gardener. He further developed the walled garden and landscape around the Mansion House that he renamed 'Thornliebank House'.

In the early years of their involvement in the area, the works at Newfield was in the hands of John's sons, Alexander (1757-1808) and James (1760-1838) under the firm Alex & James Crum & Co.

Following Alexander's death in 1808, his sons Walter (1796-1867) and John (1795-1858) came of age. Under the firm of John & Walter Crum & Co, they took over Newfield and Thornliebank works in the late 1820s by which time their uncle James Crum had paid off his debts.

James Crum ceased to be a partner in the business in 1843 and, following John's death in 1858, Walter was the only son left involved in the business. Following Walter's death in 1867, his eldest son Alexander took over the business, which finally became the Thornliebank Company Ltd. When Alexander died in 1893, the value of his estate was nearly £106,000. In 1899 the company, now with Walter Graham Crum as one of the directors, along with over 40 other printers in the areas of Manchester and Glasgow, became part of The Calico Printers Association Ltd. The calico printworks in Thornliebank closed in 1930 but the engraving department continued until 1940.

The Crum Family Timeline

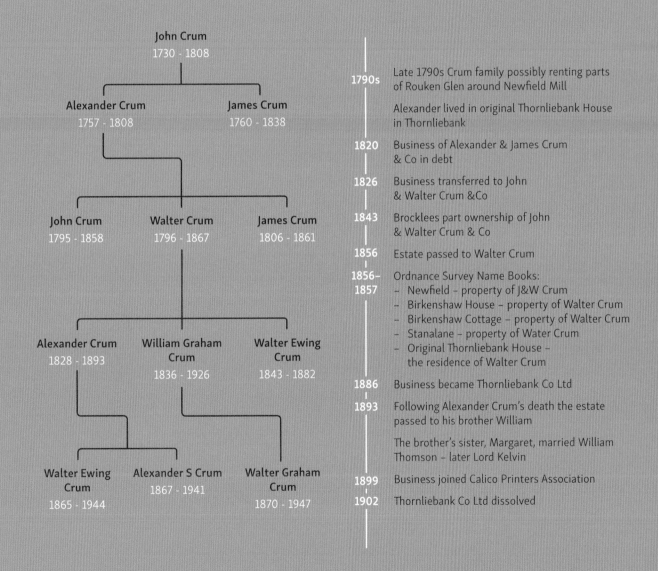

John Crum
1730 - 1808

Alexander Crum
1757 - 1808

James Crum
1760 - 1838

John Crum
1795 - 1858

Walter Crum
1796 - 1867

James Crum
1806 - 1861

Alexander Crum
1828 - 1893

William Graham Crum
1836 - 1926

Walter Ewing Crum
1843 - 1882

Walter Ewing Crum
1865 - 1944

Alexander S Crum
1867 - 1941

Walter Graham Crum
1870 - 1947

1790s Late 1790s Crum family possibly renting parts of Rouken Glen around Newfield Mill

Alexander lived in original Thornliebank House in Thornliebank

1820 Business of Alexander & James Crum & Co in debt

1826 Business transferred to John & Walter Crum &Co

1843 Brocklees part ownership of John & Walter Crum & Co

1856 Estate passed to Walter Crum

1856– 1857 Ordnance Survey Name Books:
- Newfield – property of J&W Crum
- Birkenshaw House – property of Walter Crum
- Birkenshaw Cottage – property of Walter Crum
- Stanalane – property of Water Crum
- Original Thornliebank House – the residence of Walter Crum

1886 Business became Thornliebank Co Ltd

1893 Following Alexander Crum's death the estate passed to his brother William

The brother's sister, Margaret, married William Thomson – later Lord Kelvin

1899 Business joined Calico Printers Association

1902 Thornliebank Co Ltd dissolved

Estate Buildings

in the park

During the life of the park, as people have come and gone, so have its buildings. Discover the buildings that still remain and the ones that have been lost.

Discover the parks buildings

*The clock above the arch at
Birkenshaw Cottage and the stables
Map Flag 35*

Before Rouken Glen Park opened, apart from Newfield Textile Works, there were three other main groups of buildings within the bounds of the park. These were Deaconsbank Farm, Brocklees Farm, and the Mansion House. By the 1890s a further six gate houses or lodges had been built, occupied by estate staff.

Deaconsbank Farm did not become part of the park until 1913. Brocklees Farm was occupied from the 1820s by Dugald Bannatyne, Postmaster of Glasgow, who by this time owned most of the Barony of Eastwood. Apart from Brocklees, his land included parts of Crosslees farm. It was from this time that the old farm steading of Brocklees began to be transformed into a country retreat. Its name was changed from Brocklees to Birkenshaw (or Birkinshaw) Cottage. The Birkenshaw name is a source of confusion, as there was already another farm in Eastwood named Birkenshaw (near the modern Williamwood Railway Station), plus another Birkenshaw Cottage, to the north of what is now Rouken Glen Road, in the 1850s.

Although usually called a 'cottage', Birkenshaw was quite a substantial country house. Adverts from the 1840s describe it as having a dining room, drawing room and five bedrooms, together with servants' rooms. It also had a stable, coach house, and gardener's cottage. Attached were five acres of pasture land and an 'avenue and grounds laid out with much taste'. An advert in 1844 describes Birkenshaw as:

'This beautiful Cottage, built only a few years ago, and finished with great taste, is in first-rate order, and is in the midst of Shrubbery and Planting, with romantic and retired walks on the banks of the classic Glen'.

1839

John Smith buys Birkenshaw

John Smith, a Glasgow builder, whose family had been living in Birkenshaw since 1836 bought the estate in 1839. Living alongside him in Birkenshaw Cottage in 1841 was his son James Smith (architect and builder) and his wife, and twin daughters Betsy and Madeleine. Madeleine became infamous following her trial in 1857 for the poisoning of her Jersey-born lover, Pierre Emile L'Anglelier, with whom she had been in a clandestine relationship. Madeleine was found not guilty of poisoning and 'not proven' of murder.

1843

Smith to Slater

Ownership of much of Brocklees passed from the Smiths to John Slater, a merchant. Slater was living in Birkenshaw Cottage by 1848. The cottage then seems to have been rented out, passing from Frederick Perman, a cotton goods merchant (1851), to James Robertson, manager of the Union Bank (1853). By this time most of Brocklees farm had passed into the formal ownership of the Crum family.

Birkenshaw Cottage

Park Lodge Houses

The park lodge houses have been home to estate staff and park employees.
More recently they have been converted to business use.

Top Left - *Birkenshaw Cottage and stables c1910.*

Top Right - *Birkenshaw Cottage c1986*
Map Flag 35

Bottom Left - *Unidentified park lodge house c1906*

Bottom Right - *Both the remaining original estate lodge houses in the park have been substantially altered and converted for business use.*
Map Flag 39

Highlights of Rouken Glen Park
The Mansion House

It is not known exactly when the Mansion House was built.
It is likely that plans were developed to build a larger house
when John Smith bought the estate in 1839.

Above Left - *Entrance hallway to the Mansion House c1920*

Above Right - *The Mansion House, Rouken Glen c1910 (also known as Thornliebank House). West view of the house.*

Opposite - *Two views of Thornliebank House taken from a Glasgow Park's Department Noticeboard c1955*

Left - *South side of the house overlooking the Glen*
Right - *North side of the house*
Map Flag 23

Over the years, the Mansion House in the park has had several names, which have still not been fully untangled. Built some time before the 1840s, and backing directly onto the Glen, the Mansion House was initially called 'Birkenshaw Cottage' to distinguish it from the original farm steading renamed 'Birkenshaw'. By the 1850s the names had been swapped and the mansion house was Birkenshaw House with the farm steading called Birkenshaw Cottage. The mansion was enlarged by architect Charles Wilson from 1858. In the 1871 Census 'Rooken House' is recorded as having 35 rooms with one or more windows (many times the size of Birkenshaw Cottage).

In the 1881 Census the mansion house is known as 'Thornliebank House' and has increased in size to 46 rooms with one or more windows.

By 1856 the estate and Mansion House had passed to the Crum family. By the late 1870s, the name of the mansion was changed a third time to Thornliebank House, when the Crums finally took residence. For the previous 80 years, the Crums had lived at another 'Thornliebank House' within their Thornliebank works (now the site of Spiersbridge Business Park). This older house was described in 1820 as the 'Mansion House, offices and garden of Thornliebank'.

In the 1870's Alexander Crum engaged the architect Alfred Waterhouse to enlarge the mansion house to include, amongst other works, the addition of the carriage porch or 'porte-cochere'. In the same period stables, a lodge and cottages were also built. Following the works to the mansion house, Alexander Crum renamed it 'Thornliebank House'.

Alfred Waterhouse – an acclaimed architect, who designed the town hall in Manchester and the Natural History Museum in London, received several commissions in Scotland during this period and Alexander Crum also commissioned him as architect for Thornliebank School.

By the 1870s, estate staff lived in six other properties associated with the Mansion House, including two entrance lodges and four estate cottages which housed the gardeners, a shepherd and domestic staff. The Crums also owned the farm steading and land called Stanalane on what would become the northern edge of the park.

Thornliebank House and its lands were advertised in 1894, following the death of Alexander Crum: 'The Mansion House is a handsome residence erected and altered at large cost. It contains 7 public rooms comprising: on the main floor – dining room, drawing room, library, billiard room, breakfast room, business room, corridor with entrance hall and on the upper floor – boudoir and 16 bedrooms, 4 with dressing rooms. There is ample servants' and other accommodation including wine and beer cellars, with heating apparatus on the basement floor under the house. The 'offices' (probably Birkenshaw Cottage) comprises gardener's and coachmen's houses, stabling for 12 horses with 2 large boxes, coach house, harness room, workshop, laundry, washhouse, etc. There is also a walled garden with a large range of vineries and conservatory, forcing house, potting sheds'.

A guide to the parks of Glasgow mentions the arched portico (carriage porch) at the entrance to Thornliebank House that provided cover for carriages in wet weather. The portico had the following inscription above the archway 'Dominus custodiat introitum tuum et exitum tuum'. This translates as 'The Lord guards your comings and your goings' or 'May the Lord watch over your entrance and exit'. This seems to have been fairly common message above doorways and entrances to churches.

Boundary of Rouken Glen Park on 1st Edition Ordnance Survey Map

The first Ordnance Survey map of Rouken Glen, surveyed 1856/58 & 1863, shows that Brocklees Farm steading has been redeveloped and renamed Birkinshaw Cottage. Further south, on the edge of the Glen, a much larger mansion, Birkenshaw House has been built and there has been tree planting around both the Cottage and the Mansion.

Newfield cotton mills appear in the Glen to the north of Birkinshaw Cottage. The large dam at Newfield is shown on the burn, allowing water to be stored to power the mills. A row of mill workers cottages have been built along the Paisley to East Kilbride Road to house some of the workers.

1867

Despite the vast scale of the works relative to the modest burn, when Alexander Crum took over in 1867, he was determined to continue to rely exclusively on water power. This was partly to avoid air pollution, including smuts from the chimneys affecting his textile printing. To increase water storage, he added further reservoirs at Pilmuir in Newton Mearns. He also bought Greenfield and Wellmeadow bleachfields upstream at Newton Mearns, which had been causing pollution. It is likely that he also made alterations to Newfield Dam.

Right – Birkenshaw Cottage and The Mansion House, Ordnance Survey 1856-58

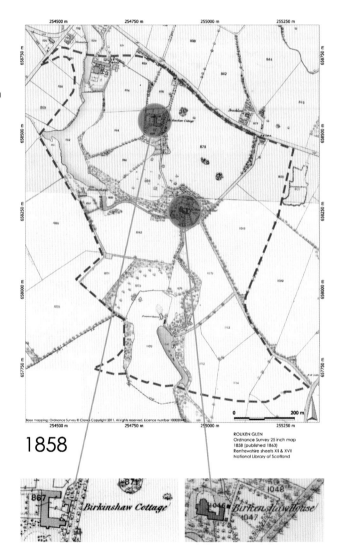

1858

ROUKEN GLEN
Ordnance Survey 25 inch map
1858 (published 1863)
Renfrewshire sheets XII & XVII
National Library of Scotland

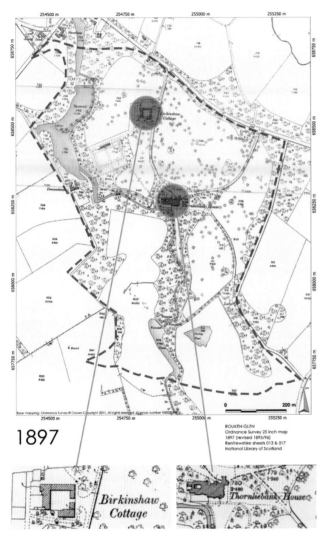

1897

ROUKEN GLEN
Ordnance Survey 25 inch map
1897 (revised 1895/96)
Renfrewshire sheets 013 & 017
National Library of Scotland

Boundary of Rouken Glen Park on 2nd Edition Ordnance Survey Map

Less than a decade before the park is opened, the boundaries of the park, can be seen on the Second Edition Ordnance Survey map (revised 1895/96 & published in 1897).

By this time, industry within the park boundary has declined. There are no longer any buildings at Rouken mill. The buildings at Newfield, and many of its associated cottages have disappeared. Due to its situation down in the Glen, Newfield had limited space to expand, and ultimately the owners preferred to consolidate their works at Thornliebank, a short distance downstream.

Big changes have also been made to the dams and water supply at Newfield to supply Thornliebank works. The dam has been rebuilt and a huge new reservoir created, with a lade alongside, which survives today.

Woodland belts have been planted to screen the estate from surrounding areas. Around 20% of the estate has been planted with trees.

Birkenshaw House has changed its name to Thornliebank House and both it and Birkenshaw Cottage have been redeveloped and increased in size. A walled garden has been built to supply vegetables to the Mansion House. There is no farming taking place within the boundary of Rouken Glen. The land is now being used wholly for leisure purposes, with the planting of many more trees and the development of a curling pond.

Left - Birkenshaw Cottage and The Mansion House, Ordnance Survey 1897

Archaeology of the Mansion House

Archaeology Scotland investigated the location and remodelling of Thornliebank House through excavation. Today the area is level and grassed over. The only features on the site are the wooden pagoda from the Garden Festival, and a surviving staircase and wall at the Glen.

Working with local volunteers, several trenches were opened over the area of Thornliebank House. These revealed substantial walls; the foundation of a large and impressive fireplace; internal brick walls, floor boards and white marble used for decoration. It was also clear that a great deal of material-including soil and clinker, had been brought into the site to level the ground surface after demolition of the house. The best find of the dig was a decorative lock fitting.

Left - Archaeology Scotland excavation of the former Thornliebank House site in September 2013.

Above - Retaining wall and staircase on the south side of the Thornliebank House site
Map Flag 23

Landscape
of the park

The park's landscape has changed greatly during its history but the one thing that has remained consistent is its breathtaking beauty.

Discover the park's landscape

The floral borders inside
The Walled Garden
Map Flag 04

Left – *Colourful rhododendron,.*

Top Right – *Lime trees lining the path next to the Events Area 2016*
Map Flag 03

Bottom Right – *Lime trees along path at the south end of the Events Area 2014*

From the 1850s Walter and Alexander Crum's landscaping focused on the Mansion House. It was built set well back from what is now Rouken Glen Road, close to a sharp bend in the Auldhouse Burn.

By the late 19th century the area was transformed by the addition of groups of trees in clumps and roundels to form a parkland setting for the house, when viewed from the public road. The horseshoe carriage drive was introduced, terminating in lodge gatehouses.

Mapped details, remnants of iron post and rail fencing alongside the drive, planting, and tree groupings, suggest that cattle may have been introduced into the landscape at some time to complement the rural aspect.

Only a very limited ornamental garden appears to have been retained immediately around the house. The main design feature was the opening of a view down a sloping stretch of land to the Auldhouse Burn. This was situated so as to give direct sight of the Glen from the principal entertaining rooms of the mansion.

Although the Glen had long been noted as a beauty spot, paths and bridges were developed alongside the burn crossing to exploit the dramatic interest provided by the situation. Another path from the Mansion House followed the Glen along the burn then climbed a flight of ornamental stairs that led to the walled garden. A 'designed' landscape had been created with relatively modest expense. The arrangement of these walks provided added interest to a stroll amid nature and well out of sight of the mansion or surrounding industry.

On a wider basis, trees were planted along the paths and the boundaries of the estate. In particular, the planting of limes delineated the main avenues.

Other trees were planted to create a parkland effect, with heavily wooded areas consisting of long lived species such as Oak, Beech, and Elm. Non-native species have been added for many reasons, including autumn colour, diversity, and to introduce new wildlife and ecosystems. Non-native trees were also introduced to combat pests and diseases. The introduction of a small arboretum south of the walled garden with a wide range of specimen trees was introduced in the late 1990s, and is something that can be added to in the future. The ground flora in certain areas hints that the park was once an area of ancient woodland of Oak, Ash and Elm. Dutch elm disease in the late 1980s resulted in the loss of hundreds of trees in the park and the 1999 Boxing Day storm felled over 150 mature trees. In the 1990s mixed tree planting took place along the railway line in the south west of the park and also more recently along the north edge of Davieland Road.

Left - Copper beech, both Spring 2016

Right - One of several Sequoiadendron giganteum or giant redwood in the park

Highlights of Rouken Glen Park
Glen Walks

The Glen Walks were developed by the Crum family. One pathway was introduced to take visitors to the upper waterfalls where the main cascade could be seen in comfort and safety.

From the terrace next to the house, a lower path ran beside the burn, then crossed over to give a view of the geological structures known as the Orchard Beds. The path then re-crossed the burn only to cross yet again to lead to the remains of the historic Rouken Mill. The arrangement of these walks provided added interest to a stroll amid nature and well out of sight of the Mansion House or surrounding industry.

Top Left - *Crossing the Auldhouse Burn in the Glen c1906*

Bottom Right - *The path from the Glen Folly c1910*

Right - *Junction of upper and lower Glen paths, left c1910*
Map Flag 16

Highlights of Rouken Glen Park

The Folly

The Folly in Rouken Glen is often mistaken for Rookend Mill from which Rouken Glen Park takes its name.

The Folly is a 19th century construction. The building hid a pump supplying water to Thornliebank House from the Auldhouse Burn and may have been driven by a waterwheel or a hydraulic ram pump. The building was made to look like a romantic ruin so that it was pleasing to the eye of visitors walking in the Glen.

Above – The man in the picture is said to be Mr Whitton, the Glasgow Park's supervisor when Rouken Glen was gifted to Glasgow Corporation in 1906.

The photograph is incorrectly labelled. It is not the old Rockend Mill but Rouken Glen Park's Folly.

Top Right – Folly and bridge 2015
Bottom Right – Folly remains 2014
Map Flag 17

Highlights of Rouken Glen Park

The Walled Garden

The other significant feature of the designed landscape was the construction of a walled garden to the northwest of the house. It could be approached either directly from the house or by a walk constructed in the valley along the burn, then climbing a flight of ornamental stairs to reach a gateway to the garden entry.

Though such gardens had often been used principally to provide food for the house, the extent to which this garden was used for vegetable production is uncertain.

The walled garden of Thornliebank House has its southern side closed only by an ornamental gate and iron railings between fine stone piers. The path beside this open aspect of the garden was flanked on the other side by a raised area accessed by ornamental steps and providing two raised beds. Whilst open sided walled gardens on sloping sites will allow cold air to flow out of the garden and minimise the development of a deep frost pocket, this garden is all on the level and it is probable that its purpose was mainly for ornamental planting, with perhaps fruit grown against the three red brick walls. Test pitting by Archaeology Scotland in the walled garden uncovered the remains of a long forgotten glass house. This would have been used to grow exotic fruits.

Although dating mainly from around the turn of the 19th to 20th century, all known photographs of the walled garden area illustrate ornamental planting. This layout would seem to be consistent with the views from the mansion being designed to see either the rolling parkland in front of the house or the dramatic gorge behind.

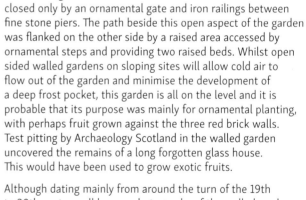

Top Left - Outside the Walled Garden c1910
Top Right - Walled Garden c1990

Middle Left - Walled Garden c1979
Bottom Left - Walled Garden c2015
Map Flag 04

20th Century
in the park

From the park's beginnings, through its temporary closure in 1983, the 20th Century was an eventful hundred years in Rouken Glen's history.

Discover the main events of the 20th Century

The Boathouse at the edge
of the Boating Pond
Map Flag 32

1900

Curling at Rouken Glen

Although the origins of curling are not fully known, there is evidence of the game being played in Scotland in the 16th century. Curling became a very popular sport in Scotland between the 16th and 19th centuries as the climate provided good ice conditions every year.

Above - Curling at Rouken Glen c1900

1903

Whitecraigs Train Station Opens

Whitecraigs Station opens as part of the Lanarkshire and Ayrshire Railway, an independent railway company, built to provide the Caledonian Railway with a shorter route from the Lanarkshire coalfields to Ardrossan Harbour.

Later the line becomes part of the Glasgow suburban train network and train timetables often referred to the station as Whitecraigs for Rouken Glen Park. Whitecraigs Station is located just outside the park at the southeast entrance.

1903 Beginnings of The Park

In a letter to the Lord Provost of Glasgow, written at Thornliebank House, Archibald Cameron Corbett, MP for Glasgow Tradeston from 1885 to 1911, informs The Corporation of the City of Glasgow that he is purchasing 136 acres of Thornliebank Estate from the Crum family, including Thornliebank House, all for £30,000. He intends personally to gift this land to the Corporation as a public park.

Dear Lord Provost,

I had a very pleasant interview to-day with representatives of the Hutchesons' Hospital Committee, who contemplate acquiring the portion of Thornliebank estate which is less suited for park purposes and more suited for feuing, and they thought it desirable that as they could no longer keep my plans private, I should intimate to you, more or less officially, that I was purchasing the part of Thornliebank estate, amounting to about 136 acres, including the house and Glen, which seems to be suited for such a purpose, with a view to handing over the property to the Corporation as a public park. It will be about two years before the new house further out, at Rowallan, is ready for occupation, so that some time will necessarily elapse before my plans can be completed. I also reserve to myself the right of deciding to what purpose the house should ultimately be put in the public interest but, as we are alike concerned that nothing should be done to impair the amenity of the park, we are not likely to differ as to the best use to which the house should be put.

My usual provision against the sale of liquor would apply to this transfer

Yours very truly,

A. Cameron Corbett

At the council meeting on 1st October 1903 the Lord Provost records 'their sense of gratitude and appreciation', which was carried by 'acclamation'.

Prior to the park opening, paths were repaired and widened, the stables at Birkenshaw Cottage converted to a ladies room and a bathroom was installed in the foreman's house.

1906

Corbett's gift – Rouken Glen

Corbett's gift to the Corporation of Glasgow is formally recorded on 2nd July 1906. The park is given the name 'Rouken Glen' to distinguish it from the rest of the Thornliebank estate.

Left *- Archibald Cameron Corbett, 1st Baron Rowallan and his son Thomas Godfrey Polson Corbett, 2nd Baron Rowallan, 1911*

Although the park is formally opened in 1906, Corbett had allowed public access to the area before this. The park was open 2 days per week on a Wednesday and Thursday. This was thought to have been done to provide limited public access, but to prevent large numbers of visitors using the park before the official opening. A postcard sent in 1905 showing part of the Glen, reads, 'The Glen is a beautiful place. Thousands of people all enjoying themselves well'.

Highlights of Rouken Glen Park

Postcards

In the days before telephones and email, postcards were a popular form of communication.

In 1894 the Post Office agreed to the private publication of postcards for use through the mail, with an adhesive stamp. By 1902, cards had been published featuring the Boer War and royal events, and in that year, the Post Office allowed both an address and message to be written on one side of the card, freeing up the whole of the other side for the picture. Britain thus became the first country to introduce the 'divided back' postcard format we are familiar with today. By this time too the size of cards had been largely standardised.

In the early 1900s, postcards exploded in popularity and they quickly became the standard medium for transmitting short messages. They were cheap and reliable, with up to seven postal deliveries a day in some areas. It was possible for a card to be posted and delivered on the same day. People bought them to keep as souvenirs as well as to send to friends. Millions of postcards went through the postal system every week.

In ROUKEN GLEN

In the days before colour photography, black and white photographs would
be hand painted in colour and then reproduced as postcards. Many of the surviving
photos of Rouken Glen Park are from postcards.

Highlights of Rouken Glen Park

The Formal Park Opening in 1906

Prior to the opening, the Lord Provost hosts a banquet at Glasgow City Hall for about 250 guests, including a party of 25 from Lyon in France. The guests travel to the park on tramcars 'decorated in French and British colours'.

Above - The Official Opening of Rouken Glen Park in 1906. The Mayoress of Lyon is wearing the light dress.

Right - The three oak trees that may be the ones planted at the opening ceremony in 1906.

At the Opening Ceremony for Rouken Glen Park on Saturday 26 May 1906, Lord Provost Bilsland of Glasgow Corporation presents Archibald Cameron Corbett with a golden key as a souvenir of the occasion. Cameron Corbett unlocks the gate, while the pipe band of the Glasgow Highlanders play a stirring march, and the party walk down the avenue to the Mansion House. A large crowd follows the guests to a railed off enclosure where 4 oak trees are planted in front of the Mansion House by Cameron Corbett, the Lord Provost, the Mayor of Lyon (who, with his wife, is on an official visit to Glasgow), and the Convener of the Parks Committee.

Loud cheers are raised as the trees are planted and the band of the 1st Lanarkshire Royal Garrison Artillery Volunteers play the National Anthems of Britain and France. There are then three cheers for Cameron Corbett. After the ceremony the party walk in the Glen. A tram service runs every two minutes from the city to the park during the afternoon and the park is crowded into the evening.
(Glasgow Herald and Scotsman - both 28 May)

Three oak trees still grow in the area where the planting ceremony may have taken place on 26 May 1906.
It is not known what happened to the fourth oak tree.

Enjoying the Land: A Park for the People

The layout of the new park incorporated the designed landscape that had evolved over the previous century for use as a country retreat. The park, with its open spaces, picturesque waterfall and wooded Glen, quickly becomes popular with visitors from Glasgow and the surrounding area - especially on Saturdays and Sundays.

When Rouken Glen Park first opens to the public, 80% of the British population are working class and the average working week is 54 hours. Promenading in the park in 'one's Sunday best clothes' is a popular free activity. Rouken Glen Park is a popular destination, out in the countryside, approximately eight miles from Glasgow's George Square, and away from the overcrowded housing in the centre of Glasgow.

Highlights of Rouken Glen Park
Lovers' Walk

Lovers Walk, Rouken Glen, Thornliebank.

The original boardwalk which formed part of the Lovers' Walk may have been constructed for the opening of the park.

The metal supports for the boardwalk are made from old tram rails. The boardwalk seems to have fallen into disrepair by the 1940s. The reconstructed boardwalk opened in 2016.

Local resident May Fabiani donated a postcard (above) with a ha'penny stamp, from one gentleman to another gentleman and postmarked 1907. The message reads 'Many thanks for the PC. I spent my holidays at Edinburgh and enjoyed it very much. Kindest regards R .M. Montgomery' at the end, it asks, 'So what do you think of this place?'

Left – Lovers' Walk c1906
Right – Lovers' Walk c2016
Map Flag 18

Opposite – Tram at the entrance to the park c1906

Transport to the Park

The Caledonian railway arrives at Spiersbridge in the 1850s. Initially a coal depot, the terminus grows into a large goods station, with multiple tracks.

Despite being so close to Rouken Glen, the station is never upgraded for passenger use, and remains purely an industrial siding, serving Thornliebank works.

In 1906 Glasgow Corporation Tramways announces a new open-topped tram line extension to Rouken Glen, via Pollokshaws, Thornliebank, and Giffnock. Before the days of widespread car use, the majority of the population rely on public transport. The Glasgow tram network is extended to the park's main entrance on what is now Rouken Glen Road. On Sunday afternoons and evenings the service frequency is every two minutes.

A second tram company, The Paisley District Tramway Company also extends its system, this time from Barrhead to Spiersbridge. A Tea Garden is added to the terminus in 1910. Initially the Paisley line is not linked to the Glasgow Tramways service to Thornliebank.

The park is on the doorstep of the large dyeing and bleaching works of Thornliebank. However, like the residents of the Mansion House before them, visitors are not put off by a few chimney stacks at Thornliebank works, visible from the park's higher ground.

1906

Tea Room Opens

A five-year lease is granted to Mr Walter M George by Glasgow Corporation for the stable buildings at Birkenshaw Cottage, to be used as a tea and refreshment hall.

1907

Plans for Tea and Refreshment Rooms

Glasgow Corporation's Parks Committee reject the use of the Mansion House as a home and school for disabled children. Plans are made to make the first and second floors 'tea and refreshment rooms'. The stables adjacent to Birkenshaw Cottage are also converted into a tea room.

1908

Freedom of Glasgow for Archibald Cameron Corbett

Archibald Cameron Corbett is granted the Freedom of Glasgow for his gifts of Rouken Glen Park in 1904 and Ardgoil Estate, Argyll in 1905 to Glasgow Corporation. Rouken Glen Park is his only land gift still used and owned as originally intended by him.

The citation reads: On 21 January Archibald Cameron Corbett, Esquire, Member of Parliament. 'In recognition of his signal* service to the City as one of its representatives in Parliament since 1885, and of his splendid generosity and lofty civil spirit in giving to the Corporation for the recreative use of the citizens, the two extensive properties known as Rouken Glen Park and Ardgoil Estate'.

*Distinguished

1909

Facilities for the park

Glasgow Corporation discuss a recommendation to build a bandstand at Rouken Glen. The estimated cost is £450 and it is suggested that unemployed Glasgow ratepayers be engaged for parts of the work. (Scotsman 8 December)

Further facilities follow, including fountains; a pavilion; a curling pond (later the boating pond); and a pitch and putt, to name a few.

In 2015 Archaeology Scotland investigated several of these features, including the pitch and putt course (as part of a walkover survey of the park), and the boat house (now a café) through a 'standing building survey'. This was done with the help of students from the University of Glasgow, University of Strathclyde and local volunteers. The walkover survey identified that traces of the pitch and putt still remains but are now grassed over. The traces can be seen to the south of the skate park.

1910

Pavilion Erected

The Pavilion is erected for use during picnics. Until 2000, it contained tables and benches for park visitors, especially children's outings, to use during wet weather.

1911

Lord Rowallan

Archibald Cameron Corbett, who gifted Rouken Glen to the public, becomes Lord Rowallan, named after his estate in Ayrshire.

First Flight Over Rouken Glen

Mr W Smith a Scottish Aviation Company pilot at Barrhead, makes a trial flight in a Bleriot monoplane, fitted with a Gnome 50 hp engine, covering a distance of about five miles at a high speed, and landing safely with a steep controlled dive. The monoplane passes over Rouken Glen at an altitude of about 1,500 feet. (*Scotsman 24 June*)

Opposite Top - Birkenshaw Cottage Tea Room c1910

Opposite Bottom - Organ (or Music Room) Tea Room, Thornliebank House c1915

Above - Pitch and putt course c1920 Map Flag 24

1913

Land Purchased for Golf Course

Glasgow Corporation purchases land at Deaconsbank for use as a public golf course. Deaconsbank Farm was situated south of the Newfield dam, between the duck pond and the golf course. It was originally part of the estate of the Maxwells of Nether Pollok. To protect the park's amenity, and to provide better access, 12 acres of Stanalane in the northwest were also added to the park in 1913. This increased the park's area to 220 acres.

Zoological Garden for Rouken Glen

In April the Glasgow Town Council discusses a report from the Parks Committee for the establishment of a zoological garden at Rouken Glen. James Whitton, Superintendent of Parks, submits a report on 11 April on his inspection of zoological gardens on the Continent and comments on the benefits to the local population, particularly the 'educative interest of such institutions'. He believes that the 'various animals and specimens' should not be confined to a limited area as 'is often the case in zoological collections which are conducted is this country for purposes of private gain'. The Scottish Zoological Society is progressing a zoological garden in Edinburgh (this would open in July 1913).

The Labour councillors are the sole opponents of the scheme which will be financed by a grant from the Common Good Fund. Councillor Wheatley argues that 'it would be more creditable to the Council if the animals were housed in the Cowcaddens and the workers were housed in the country'. Councillor Anderson, the principal supporter of the scheme, dismisses the criticisms and denies bringing the scheme forward due to the one for Edinburgh. He also reports that the tramways department could give a contribution of £20,000 as a result of the extra traffic the zoo would create.

The meeting decides by an overwhelming majority to proceed with the establishment of the zoological gardens. Mr E H Bostock presents a pair of Indian Zebu cattle to the Corporation in October for the zoo. The outbreak of war in 1914 stops any further development of the zoo. (*Scotsman & Courier 18 April, Glasgow City Archives, & Daily Record 28 May 1914*)

Rouken Glen During WW1

1914

Belgian refugees

Arrangements are made to transfer Belgian refugees living in various temporary accommodations in Glasgow. The women and children residing at Rouken Glen Mansion House are to be moved to other homes and the accommodation provided for men. An appeal for boots and clothing is issued. (*Scotsman 3 November*)

Local resident William Brown remembers working in the Thornliebank Printworks alongside some of the Belgian refugees. Working hours were 6am until 5.30pm with a breakfast and a dinner hour.

***Above** - Rouken Glen Entertainers 1914*

1915

Glasgow Cripple Children Entertained

The annual entertainment given by Glasgow Corporation to the mentally and physically defective school children in the city takes place in Rouken Glen. The weather is ideal and 3,222 children are conveyed in special tramcars to the Glen. A total of 345 teachers and members of the Boys' Brigade attend to children, all arrangements made by a special Corporation committee, assisted by representatives of Glasgow, Govan and Cathcart School Boards. 280 Infants are entertained in the schools. The children receive cakes, sweets, oranges and milk, while Punch and Judy shows, performances by the Mossbank Industrial School Band, pipers, dancers, and the Rouken Glen Entertainers add to the outing enjoyment.
(Scotsman 19 June)

Rouken Glen Illustrated

In his book 'Rouken Glen Illustrated', Thomas Macintosh notes that different areas of the park have field names:

The Front Field is the area that becomes the main car park. The Front Park is the area within the horse-shoe shaped main avenue containing the Pavilion. The Crown Field is the area that will become the pitch and putt. The Clump Field (so called because it contains clumps of three or four trees) is the area that will become the Events Area. The Upper Meadow is the area behind the Rouken Glen Falls Dam between the Golf Course Road and the railway line. The Lower Meadow containing Three Bridge Valley is the area to the west of the Glen. The High Plantation is the woods on the west side of the Lower Meadow.

Macintosh describes the Millers' Yett, on the west side of the evergreen lawn south of the Mansion House. The Millers' Yett is the remains of an entrance gate on the remnants of a stone wall. This is believed to be the gateway for farmers bringing their grain for milling to Rockend Mill when the park was farmland and before pike (or toll) roads were built.

Macintosh also records that the bell in the ivy-clad turret at Birkenshaw Stables rings out fifteen minutes before the gates of the park close each day.

1916

Glasgow Corporation children's outing

The Glasgow Corporation children's outing has beautiful weather. Some 3,500 children are transported in special trams from their different schools.
(Daily Record 17 June)

Convalescing Soldiers

Local resident John Adams has recorded his grandfather's experiences in World War I. Corporal John Adams of the 9th Royal Irish Fusiliers visited Rouken Glen Park while he was convalescing from wounds at the Royal Alexandra Infirmary, Paisley. Convalescing soldiers travelled on weekly day trips by charabanc (an early form of bus, usually open topped). Corporal Adams used postcards of Rouken Glen Park to write to friends and relatives giving updates on his convalescence.

1917

Summer Concerts

A series of concerts are planned for the summer months in 1917 throughout Glasgow's Parks, they commence on 14 May with 'The Gay Gondoliers' holding a costume party at Rouken Glen bandstand.
(Daily Record and Mail 15 May)

Mansion House inspected by the Red Cross

The Mansion House is inspected by the Red Cross for possible use as a General Hospital for the wartime wounded. The building needs extensive alteration therefore the plans are dropped.

1918

The Show must go on

Although World War I continued until November 1918, regular entertainment was provided in Rouken Glen Park throughout the war. *(The Daily Record and Mail 24 June)*

Highlights of Rouken Glen Park
The Tea Gardens

Paisley District Tramway Company Manager, Fred Coutts, purchases 5 acres at the Rouken Glen terminus on which to build his long discussed tea rooms.

A large hall with seating for 700 is built where concert parties are arranged by William Dalgleish, the first lessee. Entrance tickets cost 3d or 6d, but passengers on Paisley cars have Promenade tickets free from tram conductors. These are round, the size of an old penny coin and conductors are encouraged to give them with change.

The Paisley Tramway Barrhead to Spiersbridge line terminus at Rouken Glen now has an entertainment hall, sandpit for castle building and an artificial pond for boating as well as a flower garden to complement the Tea Gardens. *(Edinburgh Evening News 1 September 1917)*

The terminus was in the area now occupied by Thornliebank Industrial Estate - just outside the park at the northwest corner.

TEA GARDENS, ROUKEN GLEN.

The Gardens, named the Queen Mary Tea Gardens, prove immediately successful and soon acquire a 'Bioscope Display' (early film projector)

CHILDRENS SANDPIT AND MODEL SHIPS
TEA GARDENS, ROUKEN GLEN.

The Gardens, named the Queen Mary Tea Gardens, prove immediately successful and soon acquire a 'Bioscope Display' (early film projector). In the pond are exhibited historic model boats purchased by Fred Coutts after the Scottish Exhibition of National History, Art and Industry 1911 at Kelvingrove where they had been moored along the River Kelvin. The Tea Gardens has fifteen models representing all stages of boat development from the coracle and Great Michael by way of HMS Victory and the Comet to the Cunarders Britannia and Lusitania. Also purchased are redundant Glasgow 'but-an'ben' single deck tramcars, the bodies of which are taken to the Gardens to form a three bedroom summer dwelling for the Coutts family. Fond memories of Boy Scouts and Boys' Brigade camps at the Garden are held by 'Paisley Buddies' – until washed out by rain and rescued with soup in the 'waggon' as the old cars were known, then rushed back home to Paisley in a special car whistled up by Mr Coutts.

Paisley District Tramway Company is taken over by Glasgow Corporation Trams in 1923 and it seems that the Tea Gardens closed a few years before this, probably during WW1.

In addition to the Tea Gardens and two tea rooms inside Rouken Glen Park at the Mansion House and Birkenshaw Cottage, The Bungalow Tea Rooms are situated outside the park opposite East Lodge near what is now Woodfarm Road.

Opposite - *Queen Mary Tea Rooms c1910*

Left - *A concert party sitting outside the Entertainment Hall at the Tea Gardens*

Right - *A model ship in the pond at the Tea Gardens. Several other models ships are situated at the back of the pond. A children's sandpit is in the foreground.*

Highlights of Rouken Glen Park
Film Making

The Ace Film Producing Company opens their new Thornliebank Studio at Rouken Glen in October 1919.

Above – Interior of Ace Film's Thornliebank Studio

The studio is in the same location as the Queen Mary Tea Gardens and may have occupied some of the Tea Garden buildings. It seems there may have been some informal or amateur film making at Thornliebank/ Rouken Glen prior to this but Scottish film records are vague on the details.

Ace Film set up the A1 Cinema College, advertising 'To discover talent and use it'. The first production part filmed at the Thornliebank Studios is 'The Harp King'- a 'five part' Scottish romance, released at the end of 1919.

The studios are taken over by The Broadway Stage and Cinema Company Limited, who release 'Football Daft', in 1921. The film is adapted from a comedy sketch by James Milligan that had toured Scottish music halls. 'Football Daft' is Scotland's first real cinematic hit, and compares favourably with 'The Harp King'.

No further films are made at the Thornliebank Studio and it is advertised for sale or let in June 1923. It is likely to have closed soon after as the Broadway Stage and Cinema Company ceased trading in 1924.

(Merz 2016)

1920s to 1950s

Regular concerts take place in the bandstand

1920s

Picnics in the Park

William Brown recalls 'Rouken Glen was a favourite place for picnics and courting. This was where he met his wife. With pits and steel works in Lanarkshire closing, many of the young girls came to the Giffnock area to go into service in the big houses and used to take the children to Rouken Glen Park where the boys would be waiting to meet them. Quite a number of local men married these maids.'

Entertainment had taken place in Rouken Glen Park on Friday 11th June 1920 and had been attended by 3,709 children and 412 teachers.

1922

Death of William Parkin

The sudden death of Mr William Parkin, curator of Ruchill Park is announced. Mr Parkin, 53, belonged to Lanark and joined Glasgow Corporation Parks Department in 1906. He was employed as head gardener at Rouken Glen for some time and then became curator there. He transferred to Ruchill Park about a year ago. (*Scotsman 14 June*)

Deaconsbank Golf Course Opens

Deaconsbank Golf Course opens an 18 hole golf course on the Deaconsbank Farm land added to the park in 1913.

1924

The Prime Minister Visits

The Prime Minister, Mr Ramsay MacDonald undertakes a number of private engagements in Glasgow including a dinner party at 7 pm in Rouken Glen Mansion House with about 200 representatives of various sections of the Labour party. (*Glasgow Evening Telegraph 24 June*)

MP Wedding at the Mansion House

George Buchanan, Labour MP for Gorbals, Glasgow marries Annie McNee, a shop assistant, in the Mansion House at Rouken Glen on Saturday. (*Courier 21 July*)

Story of a 'Parkie'

John Cooper, born in 1900 in Newton Mearns, started working at Rouken Glen Park sometime in the 1920s as a Park Ranger (Parkie).

His duties would have included opening and closing the park gates each day, litter picking and keeping order amongst the daily visitors to the park. Gardening was also amongst his varied duties together with tending to the two Clydesdale horses used in the park at the time.

His father, also called John, had worked as a fireman at the Thornliebank Calico Printworks. The family lived at 70 Main Street in one of the company's properties and John attended Thornliebank Public School. He received a Certificate of Merit on leaving the school at the age of 14 in June 1914. Samuel Cooper, a boarder, was also living with the family in 1911 and worked as a contractor's carter. John could possibly have worked with Samuel on leaving school. Due to John's experience with horses he was drafted into the cavalry on being called up for the First World War, probably in 1918.

After returning home he married Mary in 1921 and their marriage certificate records his occupation as a carter. The Valuation Roll for Eastwood for the year 1930-31 shows John as a labourer and the occupier of a house and garden in the 'Rouken stables', Rouken Glen Park. In 1925 Archibald O'Neill, a labourer, was the occupier of this house so John and his family must have moved in sometime after 1925. In 1938 John and Mary with their four daughters, Helen, Netty, Isa and Kate moved to Newfield Cottage, a larger house, that was located in the north west corner of the park near what is now Thornliebank Parish Church.

John Cooper had certainly started working for the Corporation of the City of Glasgow Parks Department by 1926 as he is in the photograph showing the removal in 1926 of the socket stone into which the shaft of the Caplerig Cross sat prior to the removal of both to Glasgow Art Galleries and Museum. The cross - originally located in a field of Holm Farm in Mearns Parish to the south of Rouken Glen, is now in the Pavilion Visitor Centre, in front of the photo with John and his colleagues!

Highlights of Rouken Glen Park
The Boating Pond

A pond is first suggested in 1921, to be constructed on the site of the existing curling pond at an estimated cost of £6,000. However by 1922 a new proposal is made. The pond would now be much bigger, around 5.5 acres, and the cost nearly doubles to £10,500.

The same happens in 1923, with the final estimate coming in higher again at £11,500 - yet this excludes the cost of a boathouse, toilets and the boats themselves. The proposal for a pond is finally voted on some 2 years after its initial suggestion. With spiralling costs, it is perhaps unsurprising that of the initial 18 voters, 9 voted for and 9 against. In 1923 the Parks Committee recommends boating at Rouken Glen Park. It was only thanks to the Chairman, who gave his casting vote that the construction went ahead.

A motor boat and rowing boats are proposed, with local firms asked to make an offer. Plans will also be required for a boathouse. *(Scotsman 24 December)*

The boating pond with three islands is constructed in 1924 by Sir Robert McAlpine. The pond is situated just below the level of the nearby dam at Rouken Falls and a sluice and pipe from the dam fill the pond with water. The pond also has an overflow back into the Glen on its north side.

In 1924 a park visitor pays one shilling for an hour's rental of a 16ft boat. The pond proves so popular that in the years that follow more boats are ordered to deal with the demand. In 1934, two motorboats are added at a cost of £159, with further rowing boats. The boathouse is eventualluy built in 1926.

In reminiscences of Rouken Glen Park, the boating pond is one of the most remembered places in the park.

Opposite - *The Boating Pond 2015*

Top Left - *Boating pond under construction with tracks laid to move the construction materials c1924*

Top Right - *motor boat c1950*

Middle - *The boating pond c19?*

Bottom - *Rowing boat and swans 1968*
Map Flag 02

Highlights of Rouken Glen Park
The Bandstands

According to the 1910 Ordnance Survey map two bandstands are present in the park: a small square one in front of the Pavilion, and a larger round one a little further south of the first bandstand.

Concert attendance is 4,510 in 1910, growing to 5,572 in 1913 and 6,789 in 1919. It is not known why the first bandstand, which may have been built for the opening of the park, was replaced within a few years. It may simply have been too small. Glasgow Corporation Minutes between November 1921 and April 1922 indicate the second bandstand is being treated for dry rot.

In 1928 a Glasgow Corporation proposal is made for a new rectangular bandstand in Rouken Glen Park. The new improved third bandstand will seat 2,200 spectators, and cost an estimated £5,000. The 1920s sees widespread investment in such 'performance stages'. Rouken Glen, like other Glasgow parks, hosts individual bands and concerts. In 1925, a total of 316 performances are seen across Glasgow by a combined audience of 980,000 people. In 1926 Rouken Glen hosts 26 performances, with a combined audience of nearly 40,000 people. The Cape Town Symphony Orchestra proves a popular choice when they are selected in 1925 to perform at Rouken Glen, providing an international culture that a typical Glaswegian may not be able to experience elsewhere. Concerts such as this one are regularly broadcast on BBC Radio.

The Scotsman reports on 7 March that the new bandstand will be completed in time for the opening of the summer season. By 16 May 1929, just one day before the opening of Glasgow Green's, the Rouken Glen bandstand opens to the public. Bandstand attendance is nearly 12,000 in its first year.

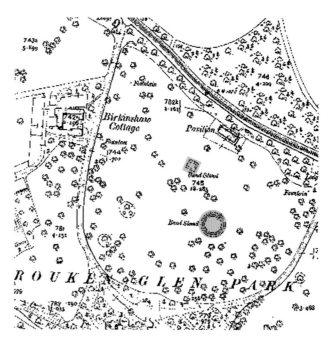

Although the bandstand has now been demolished, it once decorated the park with its relatively grand architecture and stone stepped seats. Indeed, all but one of Glasgow's bandstands has been resigned to history. The only original that remains now stands in Kelvingrove Park which underwent restoration in 2013.

Above - Bandstands, Ordnance Survey 1910

Top Left - Sketch of front of third bandstand 1930
Map Flag 30

Top Right - The third bandstand in Rouken Glen c1930

Bottom - The second bandstand incorporates a circular seating area c1910

THE BAND STAND, ROUKEN GLEN.

Late 1920s

Trams to the Park

Many children take advantage of special tram concessionary fares to travel to Rouken Glen Park. Trams run at 8-minute intervals between Airdrie and Glasgow for one penny with connections to Glasgow's southside trams. On one tram going east to Airdrie, no fewer than 66 children are on a day trip. The Monklands folk travelling in the opposite direction head for the city and beyond, as it is reported that the grounds of Rouken Glen Park are littered with pastry bags bearing the names of Airdrie and Coatbridge purveyors.
(Daily Record reminiscence 22 December 2010)

1929

Reformation Society Conference

A Scottish Reformation Society conference is held at the Mansion House, where concern is aired about the influence of the Catholic Church and the Holy See on the British Parliament.
(Courier and Advertiser 25 September)

1930s

Sunday Lock Out

Local resident Ann Crosbie remembers the swings in the park were locked up and the boats on the pond were not used until after Sunday morning church service was over.

Concerts in the Park

Local resident George Thomson who was brought up in the Dennistoun area of Glasgow, remembers concerts in Rouken Glen bandstand by music hall act Short and Dalziel, who also lived in Dennistoun. Jack Short and May Dalziel were the parents of the Scottish entertainer Jimmy Logan (1928-2001). George remembers them providing song and dance entertainment regularly at the bandstand with Jimmy joining them to dance on one occasion when he was a young boy, about 11 years old.

1930

Zoo Proposal

The question of Glasgow having a Municipal Zoo is raised again and the Parks Committee agrees in May to appoint a special committee to fully investigate the proposal. It is suggested that Mr E H Bostock's collection of wild animals could form the nucleus of a zoo. Mr Bostock, who had owned the menagerie of animals and travelled the country with them for nearly 50 years, wishes to retire and offers to sell the collection for £3,000.

In November, a meeting of the Parks Committee rejects the proposal to establish a zoo at an area in Rouken Glen occupied by a pitch and putt course. Garscube Estate and Linn Park are also investigated for a suitable site by the committee. In January 1931 Glasgow Corporation meets to decide whether to purchase Bostock's collection of animals. Councillor Kerr speaks against an enterprise in competition with the Scottish Zoo at Edinburgh and opposes it on cost grounds. Bailies Doherty and Wilson speak in favour but Councillor Kerr wins the day when the Council rejects the purchase by 41 votes to 10.

Bostock sells the whole of his stock to London Zoo and the idea of a Municipal Zoo for Glasgow finally ends. However the Zoological Society of Glasgow and West Of Scotland does open a zoo to the east of Glasgow in 1947.
(Scotsman 6 May 1930, 9 January & 21 August 1931)

1932

Natives of Glasgow Reunion

600 Glasgow expatriates from Canada and America attend an open-air 'Natives of Glasgow Reunion' gala, held in their honour in Rouken Glen Park. The visitors are conveyed to the River Clyde by the Canadian Pacific steamship, Duchess of Bedford. Several thousand people join 'lustily' in community singing in the park. The bandstand, where the 'Whoopee-makers' entertain the Scots-Canadians and their guests, is surrounded by huge crowds. A brief speech by Mr Colvin, chairman of the Canadian Committee, expresses his gratitude at the efforts made by Glasgow Corporation to give the Canadians a real Scottish welcome. Before the gala opens, spectators have an unexpected thrill when a motor car catches fire outside Rouken Glen Park. Thornliebank Fire Brigade extinguish the fire, but the car is almost completely destroyed. *(Scotsman 21 July)*

1933

Skating in the Park

Glasgow Parks Department intimates that skating is possible in some Glasgow parks including Rouken Glen. It is the first time that skating is possible on the ponds this winter. *(Scotsman 25 January)*

Local resident John Brierley recalls, 'In the 1940s and early 1950s there was always skating on the pond at some time in the winter, but this was strictly controlled and the thickness of the ice was measured carefully by Park Keepers boring the ice. The gates were locked when there was ice on the pond and only opened when the ice was declared safe. We used to climb the fence and skate if we thought there was enough ice, and there were only a few of us. When the pond was open there could be hundreds of people on the ice'.

Archibald Cameron Corbett Dies

Archibald Cameron Corbett, dies suddenly on 19 March, aged 76, while reading at the Brooks' Club in London. Apart from gifting Rouken Glen Park to Glasgow, he donated funds to many churches, missions, the Young Men's Christian Association, temperance societies, hospitals and other institutions. *(Times 20 March)*

1934

Birds Set Free in the Park

A hundred caged birds are released in Rouken Glen by the Scottish Society for the Protection of Wild Birds (RSPWB), including larks, greenfinches, chaffinches, linnets and two snow buntings. Mr John M Crosthwaite, secretary of the RSPWB frees the birds. Mrs McAuslin, a member of the Executive, said the activities of the professional bird cager ended on 28 February. In view of this, the RSPWB gave a donation to enable the Society to purchase all the caged wild birds for sale in Glasgow. This was done and the birds set free in Rouken Glen. *(Scotsman 2 March)*

1937

Boats on the Pond

John Brierley recalls visiting Rouken Glen from the age of 6. His interest was always in the boats and the pond, but it was a long walk from Clarkston to get there, so it didn't happen very often. 'When I was about 9, two friends and I, with one of our fathers, went to the Glen for an afternoon trip on the rowing boats. We were all getting into the boat, kids first, and then when the father (who was a minister) was stepping into the boat, one foot in and one foot on the quayside, his son pushed the boat out. The result was inevitable; the father went in, right in, total submersion and came back up still with his pipe firmly in his mouth. That was the end of that day's boat trip'.

Park Boundary

Glasgow Corporation attempts to extend Glasgow's city administrative and electoral ward boundary by 12,000 acres. Of the areas Glasgow requests, the Linn Park area is accepted, but Deaconsbank Golf Course, Rouken Glen Park, and Gorbals Water Works, by Barrhead, are not granted. *(Press & Journal 14 August)*. Although Glasgow Council owns Rouken Glen Park, the park has never been within the administrative boundary of the city.

1940

Seasonal Grazing

Glasgow Corporation is offering seasonal grazing at Rouken Glen Park among other locations. Also, Deaconsbank Golf Course is open for Sunday golf. *(The Daily Record and Mail on 23 March)*

WW2 1940-45
Wartime use of the Park

1940

Golf Still in Full Swing

Deaconsbank Golf Course will host the Municipal Golfers' Association's annual competition on Saturday 22 June. *(Daily Record and Mail 5 June)*

Invasion Preparation

In July, the Chief Constable of the County of Renfrew requests the removal of name-plates, direction posts, etc., in parks including Rouken Glen Park as a precaution against possible invasion. (This follows the Dunkirk Evacuation when there were fears of invasion.)

The park gatehouses are guarded by armed soldiers and Thornliebank House is being used as offices and accommodation for officers.

Wartime use of Buildings

By August 1940 the Glasgow Corporation Town Clerk reports a request to requisition sections of Rouken Glen Park such as the Mansion House, part occupied as dwelling houses by parks employees, the stable tea rooms and the public shelter (Pavilion), for military purposes.

John Brierley recalls how suddenly one day in 1940 he found the park closed except for the common area beyond the waterfall. The park gatehouses are guarded by armed soldiers and Thornliebank House is being used as offices and accommodation for officers.

In 1941 the military want to requisition the former bleach field associated with Newfield Mill. Initially Glasgow Corporation decline but the military say it is not possible to occupy the alternative area offered by the Corporation.

By 1942 further parts of Rouken Glen Park near Whitecraigs are requisitioned by the military. Compensation is agreed for the areas requisitioned in 1940-1, with the Town Clerk informing the military that no compensation will be required for the further areas near Whitecraigs if the military erect additional protection round the park to safeguard cattle and sheep grazing on the land.

Jack Cook, who served as a driver/ mechanic with the Royal Army Service Corps, recalls scrubbing the steps of Thornliebank House's huge staircase as a punishment for turning up late for parade. Ordinary personnel are accommodated in 20 Nissen huts which run from East Lodge along the Davieland Road side of the main avenue to the Mansion House. The huts are about 10 metres by five metres wide and sleep around 10 men. In the centre of each is a cast iron pot-bellied stove to keep the men warm. The quartermaster's store is at East Lodge and the Pavilion is used as the NAAFI or canteen.

Wartime use of Parkland

The army has arrived and the park becomes full of all types of vehicles - from motor cycles to buses and tank transporters, as No 7 VRD (Vehicle Reserve Depot) storage and distribution depot. Jack Cook recalls that the grassed areas in the park were like a mudbath. John Brierley also remembers the mud, and thought that the beautiful park would never be the same again. The area between the Pavilion and the Mansion House is littered with army vehicles from Bedford trucks, officers' staff cars, Humber utility vehicles, motorbikes, ambulances, small Austin and Morris 10hp runabouts.

During the war, army trucks travel from Rouken Glen Park to ports around the country to collect damaged vehicles that needed overhauled and sent back to the front. Vehicles are repaired in a large garage in the area of the park now occupied by the Pro-Soccer Football Complex. The Rouken Glen vehicle depot is a busy place with hundreds of people coming and going. In addition, vehicles also deliver mail and supplies to other army facilities throughout Scotland.

Hundreds of military personnel are stationed at Rouken Glen, and there is a large turnover. After spending three months at Rouken Glen, Jack Cook's platoon is transferred to Rochdale, before spending the rest of the war in North Africa.

Then one day in 1944, almost overnight, Rouken Glen Park is suddenly empty of vehicles. Later it was realised that the vehicles have gone south for the D-Day landings.

Left - The ATS girls and the mud in Rouken Glen

1944

Mud, Girls and Gears

The Auxiliary Territorial Service (ATS) has now taken over the servicing and maintenance of 'recce' cars – high-powered vehicles that are used for reconnaissance on all the battle fronts.

At the depot where the girls work so many cars and other vehicles pass through their hands, and the ground becomes so churned up, that they must first beat the mud before they tackle the mechanical work involved.

Adept at manipulating their vehicles – and themselves – across the deep, skiddy bogs, the girls are also highly skilled motor mechanics. They do all the running repairs on the latest army fighting vehicles. With the invasion of Europe their care and skill would be proved. *(Illustrated Magazine 11 March)*

Jack Cook who served in the park during the war, recalls that the ATS women carried out many duties including working as orderlies, drivers, postal workers and ammunition inspectors. Jack met his future wife Effie at Rouken Glen. She was a driver and regularly took part in 20-30 lorry convoys from Rouken Glen to another transportation depot in Govan. Effie initially lives with a lady who had a house on Eastwoodmains Road and was later billeted with other ATS girls in Nissen huts in Eastwood Park.

Despite most of the park being occupied by the military in 1943, *They Took A Chance – And Waited for Hours!* Queuing for the boat but not for Rothesay! – Children spending their Easter holiday waiting for paddle-boats at Rouken Glen. *(Sunday Post 25 April)*

Post War 1945

Park reopens to the Public

Glasgow Corporation is considering reopening Rouken Glen Park to the public in September, even if in a limited way, after army activity in the park ceases, with the end of the war. *(Daily Record 8 August)*

Military Use Continues

Some of the army facilities in the park continue in use for a time after the war. Local resident May Fabiani recalls that her husband did his National Service just after the war and was billeted with the Medical Core of the Black Watch in Rouken Glen Park. 'He was quite annoyed, because all his friends were going to Egypt and other exotic places, with great stories, but the extent of his travelling was only between Rouken Glen Park and Riddrie in Glasgow.'

Military use of the Mansion House

A letter from the military to Glasgow Corporation offers to transfer the electric mains cable installation from the road to the Mansion House at original cost of £150 and electric light installation in the house of about £60 15s 0d (half of original cost). (*Glasgow Corporation Minutes 29 August*)

Another letter from the military announces that Rouken Glen Mansion House, and other portions of the park containing buildings, will be released from requisition from 15 October. This excludes an area of about 12 acres in the northwest corner. (*Glasgow Corporation Minutes 10 October*)

Letter from Grace Wood, lessee of the Mansion House Tearooms, asking for continued consideration for the use of the building, after the termination of her lease pending restoration of the building following occupation by the War Department. (*Glasgow Corporation Minutes 12 December*)

1946

Reconstruction of the Park

Parks Department employees are working on reconstruction of the park. (*Glasgow Corporation Minutes 12 June*)

1947

Reclaiming the Park

Glasgow Corporation decide to purchase a number of former military buildings, including a garage and other small huts left from the War Department for £250, within the only remaining portion of Rouken Glen Park still held by military authorities – located in 12 acres in the northwest of the park. (*Glasgow Corporation Minutes 3 September*)

Work is continuing on park reinstatement with Sportworks Ltd of Glasgow offering to carry out excavation, drainage, levelling and harrowing on de-requisitioned areas at Rouken Glen Park at an estimated cost of £2,500. (*Glasgow Corporation Minutes 29 October*)

Park for the People

Post-war the park's biggest story is the ordinary folk who come to the park from all over the city of Glasgow (and by tram from Paisley) to enjoy themselves.

In the late 1940s Glasgow resident Mary Leckie travels by tramcar all the way from her home in Maryhill, direct to the gate outside the park. Mary describes how the greenery of Rouken Glen contrasted with the big tenements of Maryhill and she felt as if she was on her holidays when she visited the park.

Apart from using the trams, many visitors think nothing of walking for an hour or more to reach the park. Large groups of children are also bussed from much further afield for picnics with schools, Sunday schools, and numerous other youth organisations.

Former Rouken Glen Park gardener Hugh Nelson remembers many church outings for picnics to Rouken Glen during the summer. 'Sometimes there would be 30-40 double decker buses parked all the way down Davieland Road. The park would be sectioned off. Picnic One would be in a certain area, etc, with thousands of kids. The Saturday before the schools closed for the summer holidays would be picnic day. The children would be catered for with a bottle of ginger and a box of goodies containing a sandwich, a bag of crisps and a cake. If the weather was bad they could shelter in the Pavilion.'

Many visitors recall queuing for the rowing boats, the motor boat, and the pitch and putt. Mischief in the park was controlled by the 'Parkie' (Park Keeper). Local resident Robert Ward recalls how the Parkie was a feared man who spent a lot of time chasing kids off the grass. Another resident Rochelle Moore recollects boys getting into trouble for diving off boats and swimming to the pond islands.

The 1950s

Local resident Robert Ward remembers learning to play golf on Deaconsbank Golf Course at the age of 10 in the early 1950s and paying sixpence for a round of golf.

His wife Lena recalls another smaller house next to Deaconsbank Golf Clubhouse, which was the shepherd's house. Robert also recalls that the Clubhouse had a small locker-room and a tea room with waitresses in black outfits and white aprons. At the time Robert thought it was very posh. The Clubhouse also had a shelter which was like an old school shelter.

Another resident Roderick McDougall recalls that in post war austerity, Rouken Glen Park was somewhere to go for free, 'In the late 1950s while still at school in Thornliebank, I helped with the boats and it honed my rowing skills. It was great because we were working there and so we got on the boats for free. There were two fibreglass boats which were red while the rest were wooden in Glasgow Corporation colours. The boats were moored out at the largest island overnight. We would collect all the boats together at the end of the day, take the oars out and put them in the boat shed. Then using a fibreglass boat tow all the other boats out to be moored off the island, use the fibreglass boat to row back to the jetty, lift the fibreglass boat out of the water and put it in the boatshed. The boats were all stored in the boathouse over the winter.

Roderick remembers these boats were dual purposed. 'During the boating season the boats were all out on the pond. When the White Cart river flooded, which it did regularly at that time around Tantallon Road in Shawlands, these boats were the ones that were taken down to row people out from their houses.

There was a motor launch which did a figure of 8 trip in the pond. This wooden motor launch could take 20-30 people at a time.'

Roderick recalls at the weekends there was an ice cream machine in the Boathouse and freezer for coca cola bottles. 'One of my school friends worked the coke machine putting the coca cola bottles in one end and taking out the cold ones at the other end'.

Rouken Glen Park was somewhere to go for free

1950

Rifle Champion in the Park

Mr R J Ramsay from Irvine, is the new Scottish small-bore rifle champion, winning the Earl Haig Memorial Trophy at Rouken Glen, where the Scottish meeting of the National Small-Bore Rifle Association was held. With a score of 792 out of a possible 800, he is one point ahead of a former holder, Mr A A Smith of Glasgow Police. *(Scotsman 1 June)*

More recently when some dead or damaged trees have been felled in Rouken Glen, bullets have been found buried in the bark. Therefore it would seem that not everyone who took park in the rifle competitions was as good at hitting the targets as Mr Ramsay or Mr Smith!

Mansion House in Decline

Following its use by the military the condition of the Mansion House is in decline. Walter Guthrie Ltd submits the lowest offer to eradicate dry rot in the Mansion House's tea room and the floor above. It is debated whether to continue to use the remaining portions of the house.

The following year, it is agreed that the west wing of the mansion house should be demolished as soon as practicable. *(Glasgow Corporation Minutes 13, 27 September 1950 and 14 April 1951)*

1951

Stone arch Repair

A repair to the stone arch at the entrance to the walled garden costs £30.

Cost of Repair to Mansion House

The War Department Valuer offers a total of £4,317 11s 5d for reinstatement of the remaining parts of the Mansion House. This includes work to eradicate further dry rot, and plaster and paintwork. *(Glasgow Corporation Minutes 24 October)*

1952

Sunday School Picnic

Between 1952 and 1958, Glasgow residents Alistair and Catherine Raeburn come to the park for an annual picnic with the Socialist Sunday School – a non-religious organisation with members from Nitshill and Pollok. 'The group would leave Priesthill around 10 am taking about an hour and a half to walk to Rouken Glen. We would cut through from Priesthill, into the area we called Black Hills which was old open coal mines in Darnley. In the park the group would then set up for lunch. The tea urn was carried to the park on our backs in a sling arrangement; the group each taking turns to share the load. We heated the water for tea by sitting the urn on a camping-style primus stove. We sat right outside the Pavilion and we had our sandwich bag handed to us in a grease-proof paper poke. If it was wet we were allowed to go inside the Pavilion. After lunch we had the races, so we probably spent 3 or 4 hours in the park before walking back home.'

1953

Delay to Mansion House Demolition

There is a delay to the demolition of part of the Mansion House and a wartime Nissen hut. *(Glasgow Corporation Minutes 15 April)*

Site of Special Scientific Interest

Rouken Glen Park is recorded as a Site of Special Scientific Interest. The citation (by Scottish Natural Heritage) states:

'Rouken Glen lying just over 3km to the east of Barrhead together with Waulkmill Glen provides complementary sections in the rocks of the Upper Limestone Formation of Arnsbergian age, formed around 320 million years ago. These are the best available sites for this rock interval in the Central Coalfield-Stirling outcrops, and as such are essential stratigraphic sites. Together these sites show a section between the Index Limestones and the Calmy Limestones, each locality showing sedimentary and palaeontological differences and variations within this interval. These are key sites for studies of Arnsbergian (uppermost Lower Carboniferous) rocks in Scotland'.

1954

Missing Art

A sculpture 'Sea Maiden' is gifted to Glasgow Parks by British sculptor Charles d'Orville Pilkington Jackson, residing in Edinburgh. The Director of Parks is authorised to place the sculpture near the waterfall in Rouken Glen Park. The statue was made of Pentelic marble, and was carved using abrasive methods between 1934-5 by the artist and his assistant, Tom Bowie.

It is not known if the sculpture was installed in the park or what happened to it. (*Glasgow Corporation Minutes 6 January*)

Today, a 1938 bronze sculpture by the same artist stands in Greenbank Gardens, Clarkston.

1955

Military Buildings

Some military buildings still persist in the park. Glasgow Corporation Housing and Works Department are authorised to re-roof and supply and fit rones at a cost estimated at £459 to one of the two ex-military sheds now used for storage of mechanical plant.

The following year, a building formerly used by the Royal Electrical and Mechanical Engineers as a garage and workshop, is to be used for mechanical work presently carried out at a garage in Kelvingrove Park. (*Glasgow Corporation Minutes 17 August 1955 and 10 October 1956*)

Gospel Hall Sunday School Visit

Children from The Gospel Hall Sunday School in Bonnybridge travel to Rouken Glen Park on Saturday 11 June. They enjoy a picnic, games and races. Some decide to spend their day walking throughout the park, while others spend time on the boating pond or pitch and putt. All in all, the outing is voted a great success. (*Falkirk Herald 18 June*)

1959

Park Life

Hugh Nelson is an apprentice gardener at Rouken Glen Park. He remembers one of his first tasks in the park was to go up a ladder to prune the climbing rose on the front of Thornliebank House.

Hugh recalls, 'All the paths in the park had names. The path to the rear of Thornliebank House was the Laundry Walk. The one leading down the steps to the Glen path from Thornliebank House was the Kitchen Walk.'

Left - Walled Garden c1950s
Map Flag 04

Right - Tram approaching the corner of Spiersbridge Road and Rouken Glen Road c1950s

Hugh recalls that in 1959 a policeman used to come regularly to the park. 'The policeman was probably about a year from retirement. He would stop boys he suspected of stealing birds' eggs. He would ask the boys to take their hands out of their pockets and would then slap his hand hard against their pockets smashing the eggs.

Nothing was said, no complaints made against the boys to mums or dads and they were allowed to go with the egg yolks running down their legs.

In the 1960s and 1970s when a big event was held in the park, park staff used to call up Charlie the local police inspector and ask for a car to be sent round. A police car with its lights flashing would then drive around the park and this would calm down any excitement in the park. There was never any trouble at events.'

Hugh says there is a difference in the way Rouken Glen Park is used today compared to when he started work in 1959. 'There are generational groups today; families spend more time together on days out; it is not safe for children to cycle on roads so they now cycle in the park; the garden centre also brings in visitors and there is more public awareness of health/wellbeing. In addition, there is a larger proportion of dog owners using the park every day'.

The 1960s

1960

School Trips

Grace Smith was an infant teacher in Sir John Maxwell school in Pollokshaws in the early 1960s and visits the park with her class and with her Sunday school class from Cathcart Baptist Church. She recalls, 'There wasn't a play area in the park at that time so we would be involved in running games such as egg and spoon'.

Above - Grace Smith, back row
second left, in front of the Pavilion
c1960
Map Flag 33

1961

Treats in the Park

Local resident Ross McKemmie works in the boathouse kiosk at the boating pond during school holidays in 1961-63. 'The kiosk was on the right of the boat shed looking from the pond, with the rest of the building used to store boats. Firms had to bid for the catering rights in Glasgow parks and in 1961-62, Walls the ice cream company, won the purvey in Rouken Glen. We sold Coca Cola and other fizzy drinks, confectionery, crisps and cigarettes as well as the range of Walls ice creams and ice lollies.

The catering was controlled from the Birkenshaw Cottage tea room attached to the stables, managed by a wonderful lady called Chrissie Sloss. She was assisted by five or six local women, including her sister Mary, who was well known for the scones she baked on the premises. The tea room served light meals like pie and chips as well as tea and cakes, which I think were bought in from Cosh, the local Thornliebank baker. In 1963, Chrissie and the baker together won the purvey directly.

The stock had to be transported from the tea room to the kiosk, and often I had to push a wheelbarrow filled with bottles and confectionary all the way to the pond. This was a gardener's barrow maybe 3 x 4 feet on two wheels and fully loaded only just within the strength of a schoolboy. At the ramp just before the pond I would have to unload the barrow and carry the crates up one by one.

The area around the pond jetty could get very busy in those days with the motor boat, rowing boats and later dual hulled pedal boats, as well as the kiosk. The kiosk had an open counter maybe six feet long and customers could be three deep needing served by one or two of us behind the counter. We could turn over £60 in a decent day with Mars bars selling for 6d or 7d (2.5p) and crisps for 3 or 4d. We didn't have a monopoly. On Davieland Road there would often be 3 or 4 ice cream vans successfully competing for much the same business.'

1961

Fire damage to Thornliebank House

The Scotsman newspaper takes a photograph:
Lena Ward remembers exploring Thornliebank House when she was about 10 years old after it had been closed and was in a dangerous condition prior to demolition. She remembers what she believed to be a beautiful mural on a wall.

*Left - Thornliebank House 20 July
with roof missing due to fire damage*
Map Flag 23

1964

Sugar Ray Visits

In September the famous American middleweight boxer Sugar Ray Robinson is due to fight Irish born Mick Leahy at Paisley Ice Rink. He is staying at the local McDonald Hotel in Giffnock and uses Rouken Glen for training runs. Teenager James Bone and his friend have cycled up to Rouken Glen and are sitting by the boating pond when Sugar Ray and his trainer come jogging through the park. 'They stopped a few yards away, had a short conversation, then came over and asked if they could borrow our bicycles. How could we refuse? They explained that they were bored with running and wanted to try something different. They completed one circuit of the pond then gave up, saying it was too much like hard work.' Sugar Ray lost the bout on points after 10 rounds.

1965

Mansion House and Bandstand Demolished

An offer to demolish the bandstand at Rouken Glen Park by Samuel B Allison Ltd for £140 is accepted. An offer is also received by John Walsh to demolish the Mansion House for £1,975. *(Glasgow Corporation Minutes 3 March and 26 May)*

In 2015 Archaeology Scotland investigated the bandstand location by excavation. A small trench was excavated over the site of the second and third bandstands identifying the location through the rubble.

1965-73

Park Guides Available

Glasgow Corporation Parks Department publish visitor guides containing official programmes for all its public parks.

The 1970s

1970

Alpine House Opens

Rouken Glen Park opens a new alpine house. This is situated close to the walled garden and is open to the public from 1.30pm – 4pm every day, from mid-March to mid-October.

1971

Horse and Cart Rides

A horse and cart provides rides in the park from Birkenshaw Cottage Tea Room to the boating pond.

1973

Motorboat

A new motorboat called 'The Glen' is delivered to the boating pond. The motorboat can be swung round on a bogey at an angle for launch. About 30-40 people can be seated in the boat for trips round the pond.

Left - Skating on a frozen pond c1970   *Right - Horse and cart ride c1970*
Middle - Queuing at the boating pond c1970

1974

Red Devils Drop in on Open Day

A large crowd watch the 'Red Devils' Parachute team give a display at the Open Day in Rouken Glen Park. This is the fourth year of the Open Day and in previous years the weather has forced the cancellation of the jumps. It is a scorcher of a day and other Open Day activities include a record 80+ entries for the sheep dog trials and a children's gymkhana.
(Mercury 21 June)

1970s

The Model Steamer Club moves to Rouken Glen from Maxwell Park

The club started as a group of scratch scale model boat modellers and enthusiasts of Clyde paddle and turbine steamers. Their models rekindle fond memories for many Glaswegians.

Current members sail a more varied range of models; there are still the old favourite paddlers, but these now sail alongside the post war diesels of Caledonian MacBrayne ferry fleets, a range of puffers, lifeboats, modern war-ships and kits.

1975

The Greenhouse Nursery

Duncan Fordyce remembers in 1975-76 when he was a third year apprentice gardener, that wallflowers were grown in the Rouken Glen Park walled garden nursery/ greenhouse area and that these plants were a particular favourite for wild rabbits. One park employee used to come into the park early in the morning and sit with a shotgun pointed out the side window of the glasshouse. Any rabbits killed were then used by another park employee for his dinner that night.

The greenhouse area within Rouken Glen Park is now The Young Enterprise Scotland Academy operated by Young Enterprise Scotland.

Boundary Change

As part of local government reorganisation, Glasgow Corporation is renamed The City of Glasgow District Council. Rouken Glen Park is just outside the Glasgow boundary; when the park opened in 1906 it was within the boundary of Renfrewshire (the 'County' of Renfrew); with council re-organisation in 1975 the park is within the boundary of the newly created Eastwood District Council.

Below – *Duncan Fordyce (in the suit) talking to visitors in East Renfrewshire Council's training facility in 2008 shortly before the facility was sub-leased Map Flag 37*

Top Left – *Rouken Glen Park swings, April holiday c1920*

Top Right – *The swings in 2015 after the Heritage Lottery Funded play park refurbishment*

Above Left – *Play park climbing frame in front of the Pavilion Visitor Centre 1989*

Above Top – *The swings in 2014 before the play park was refurbished*

Above Bottom – *Infant play equipment outside Birkenshaw stables 1989*

Opposite – *The new ship's mast climbing frame 2014*

Opposite Page – *The new play park 2014*
Map Flag 05

Highlights of Rouken Glen Park

The Play Park

Children's swings have always been a feature of the park. Former Park Manager Duncan Fordyce remembers swings in the meadow and opposite the Mansion House which were removed by Eastwood District Council in the 1980s as they no longer met the required safety standards.

The present play park, in front of the Pavilion Visitor Centre, emerged in the early 1980s with a helter skelter, several climbing frames and a log-built activity frame with chute. This facility was gradually extended until 2014 when the play area and equipment were completely replaced.

In the mid-1980s a few rocking animals on springs were added for infants – spaced along the edge of the main paths. However by the late 1990s all these items had been removed as they were no longer usable.

The 1980s

1980

Sing to God

A Sing to God service is held next to Rouken Glen's Boating Pond. The service brings together churches of all denominations as part of the Many Songs – One God theme of Eastwood Festival. Songs feature the elements of earth, air, fire and water linked to faith. *(Mercury 23 May)*

Sheepdog Trials Moved

The Invitation Sheepdog Trials, organised by Glasgow District Council in Rouken Glen Park since 1970 are being transferred this year to Bellahouston Park. *(Mercury 20 June)*

1981

Sing to God

Another Sing to God service is held next to Rouken Glen's Boating Pond. The service brings together various faith groups as part of the Good Neighbours theme of Eastwood Festival. *(Mercury 1 May)*

Financial Dispute

Eastwood and Glasgow District Councils are in a financial dispute which dates back to Local Government Reorganisation in 1975. Eastwood had agreed to pay a proportion of the running costs of Rouken Glen Park. The amount has almost doubled to £28,000 in six years. Eastwood has given notice that it wishes to withdraw from the informal agreement and Glasgow is threatening legal action. *(Mercury 21 August)*

The Parks Man Power

Hugh Nelson recalls, 'From the 1950s to the early 1970s, 27 men worked almost exclusively on gardening tasks in the park. Each man had a path to maintain and all the paths in the park were edged. Five men also worked in the walled garden with two apprentices. In August each year, the apprentices moved to a different Glasgow park.

The park apprentices were trained by qualified staff and they were sticklers for tool maintenance, plant diary keeping and plant identification. At this time the gardening staff grew all the seasonal plants used in Rouken Glen Park. The facilities consisted of cold frames, one large greenhouse and a pit house for propagating. This was partly sunk into the ground and serviced by a coal fired boiler. Up until 1989 plants for the park were propagated and grown on site.'

Hidden Plans

A Glasgow Council document, which the council refuses to release, contains plans to build a hotel and housing in Rouken Glen Park. A Council spokesperson said, 'It is not a report or a secret, merely the council thinking about possibilities for the park.' The chairman of Eastwood Council's Planning Committee expresses sympathy with the plan 'A park is an item of high council expenditure. There is not so much need for a park of the size of Rouken Glen these days and I do not think the park core would be affected. It is protected by clauses in the gift contract.' *(Mercury 18 December)*

1982

Frozen Falls

Rouken Glen Park's waterfall is frozen over. *(Mercury 15 January)*

Park Activities

Rouken Glen activities include Renfrewshire Schools cross-country championships, sponsored walks by Christian Aid and the Isobel Mair School, the Eastwood Cub Scouts annual sports competition and guided walks by the Glasgow Urban Wildlife Group. *(Mercury 23 April, 28 May, 10 September and 8 October)*

1983 Closure of the Park

Park Management Transfer from Glasgow to Eastwood

In 1983 rumours began to circulate that Glasgow District Council, who had owned Rouken Glen since it was donated by Cameron Corbett in 1906, wanted to reduce the amount of money it spent in the park.

On 25 August, Glasgow District Council formally announces that it will cease to maintain Rouken Glen Park and Deaconsbank Golf Course, in a bid to save £250,000 a year. The 13 staff employed at the park are to be redeployed. Glasgow Council opposition group leader Bailie William Aitken said the decision on Rouken Glen was justified and that his group believed the land should be sold for private housing.

The Honourable John Corbett, great grandson of Archibald Cameron Corbett who gifted Rouken Glen Park to the citizens of Glasgow, has instructed his lawyers to look into the conditions attached to the gift. If there is any cash from Rouken Glen Park, Corbett wants it for his home at Rowallan Castle in Ayrshire. At this time, his Rowallan estate is being reduced in size to pay cash to the five beneficiaries of his grandfather's estate (of which he is not one). He believes that if his great grandfather's gift of Rouken Glen to the citizens of Glasgow is to be changed in any way, then Glasgow District Council should not benefit financially more than the Corbett family. *(Glasgow Herald)*

Five days later, The Herald prints six letters protesting about the proposed closure of Rouken Glen Park.

On 31 August, Glasgow Council Leader Councillor Jean McFadden says she is opposed to Rouken Glen Park becoming a housing development however there is no possibility of the Council reversing the withdrawal of park maintenance. Disposal of the park in the form of a lease for a sports facility, farmland park, or agricultural use are being investigated and the National Trust is being approached.

The Director of Parks says the park will remain open, although notices will be erected advising the public to take care because of the maintenance withdrawal. Glasgow Council state that this situation is due to Government expenditure cuts.

Council employees and local community groups are expected to stage a protest demonstration outside Glasgow City Chambers. The Glasgow Model Steamer Club has a farewell sail on the boating pond after 10 years at Rouken Glen. The pond is to be drained by the weekend. *(Glasgow Herald)*

Three days later The Mercury reported: Glasgow's shock announcement last week that they will close Rouken Glen Park in six days was made without any discussion on what will happen to the park. Glasgow Councillors only discussed the full details this week.

Reports in national newspapers imply that the threatened closure was due to Eastwood Council's refusal to pay towards the maintenance of the park which lies within the district's boundary. Although Rouken Glen Park lies within Eastwood, the Properties Commission decided that the park still belonged to Glasgow since it had been gifted to the City.

A tentative proposal that Eastwood fully maintain the park is declined as Glasgow would remain the owner. As mentioned, an informal agreement had been in place until 1980, with Eastwood paying part of the costs. Frequent press allegations that the two Councils have been arguing over the park are denied.

The Mercury mounts a 'Save the Glen' campaign with a petition published in the paper. *(Mercury 2 September)*

On the same day, The South Side News reported: The Scottish Tree Trust fears that thousands of trees and wildlife will be destroyed if Rouken Glen Park is sold to private developers.

Above - Nanette is in the front row, on the right of the lady holding the petition.

Glasgow states that no decision has been made yet about when the park gates will close. A council spokesman said that families living in the park lodges will probably stay and if this isn't the case the park will be patrolled in other ways. The spokesperson cannot give an answer to the question of what will happen to the swans living on Rouken Glen Park's Boating Pond.

Nanette Davidson, who returned to live in Giffnock in 1982 with her young family, recalls coming to the park one day and finding boulders blocking the paths. 'Rouken Glen Park was one of the main attractions of the area. So when I heard talk of the park being closed shortly after we arrived in Giffnock - I was very concerned! When Glasgow closed the park, they brought in JCBs to put boulders on paths, to stop vehicle access and prevent the park being used as a racetrack. To my horror, the gardens were 'looted' for plants and stock! My neighbour, Elma Lindsay, and I were appalled and decided action was needed. Enquiries confirmed that Rouken Glen had been gifted to the people of Glasgow, so plans to build houses on it were in my book, not on! I was angry when I then found out that the local press were alleging that the park was being used as a negotiating tool between Glasgow and Eastwood Councils.

We started a campaign and a petition to campaign against the closure and the house building. My neighbours helped look after my girls and I visited all of the local schools, playgroups, shops and businesses and collected several thousand names. I was interviewed by local press and by Bill McFarlan for STV news and I presented the petition to Eastwood's offices.'

On 6 September, a Special Meeting of Eastwood Council is held to discuss the City of Glasgow District Council's decision to close Rouken Glen Park. Council officials then meet with representatives of the City of Glasgow District Council in the City Chambers on 8 September but Glasgow is unwilling to concede ownership of Rouken Glen Park and Deaconsbank Golf Course. An offer to lease the park will be considered subject to ongoing negotiations.

A Parks Department worker seals off the helter skelter in Rouken Glen Park to stop local children from using the play facilities. (M23)

On 9 September, The South Side News reports: Outstanding Response To 'Save The Glen' Campaign.

The South Side News and its sister paper The Mercury receive over 1,000 signatures.

Eastwood is considering a proposal to accept the transfer of the park from Glasgow provided it is without major conditions or restrictions which will prevent Eastwood re-appraising park usage while maintaining maximum leisure use.

On 16 September The South Side News reported: Councils To Agree on 'Glen' Deal

Glasgow is prepared to offer a 125 year lease to Eastwood which has given a guarantee that there will be no housing development in the park. The deal allows Eastwood to sub-lease part of the park for leisure developments and change the layout to meet its own requirements.

To date 2,250 readers have signed the paper's petition to save the park.

Local resident, Dorothy McBride, recalls the park in the early 1980s just before the change of management. 'The Pavilion was only open for a couple of hours at a time when school trips used it for picnics. The walled garden seemed run down as it was not being planted to the same standard as it had been in the 1970s. I remember the horses, a black Shire-cross and a brown Clydesdale which were used for the horse and cart rides. I think they transferred to Pollok Park when Rouken Glen closed. The motor launch from the pond was also moved to another park.'

Left - A poster protesting about the closure of Rouken Glen. (9th September)

(Michael Kelly was Lord Provost of Glasgow District Council when the 'Glasgow's Miles Better' campaign was launched in June 1983 to promote tourism to the city).

Right - A Glasgow Council Parks Department workers seals off the helter skelter in Rouken Glen Park to stop children using the play facilities

1984

Eastwood District Council Takes Control

Rouken Glen Park is to officially come under the authority of Eastwood District Council on Monday 16 January when Provost Ian Robertson signs a 125 year lease.
(Mercury 13 January)

By the time Eastwood takes over maintenance, Duncan Fordyce recalls the grass is about 2 feet high and four tractors with different types of equipment are required to cut it down.

Eastwood Council sends a surveyor to Rouken Glen Park on 6 January, to evaluate the condition of the park's structures. Many, including the Golf Clubhouse and lodge houses are in very poor state due to neglect and vandalism. Many other buildings, including Birkenshaw Cottage, Birkenshaw Tea Room, and the boathouse need extensive repair work.
(Eastwood Council Minutes, 20 January)

Duncan Fordyce remembers when Eastwood took over the maintenance of the park and initially inspected the park buildings. 'The East Lodge gate house was dilapidated. The first time someone entered, the floors were so rotten that they fell through the floor. The other gatehouse had walls so soft you could push a pen into them.

'Prior to the closure of Rouken Glen Park, there was evidence that Glasgow had been withdrawing funding from the park for some time. All the fencing in the Glen had becoming dilapidated. The fencing in those days was round timber style, made of Spruce about 6 inches in diameter all peeled and nailed together. I remember two joiners working virtually full-time to maintain this style of fencing. Eastwood changed the fencing style because we would never have been able to stay on top of the maintenance.'

Park Re-development

Rouken Glen Park continues to change. The construction of Spiersbridge roundabout and the realignment of Rouken Glen Road in 1984 by Strathclyde Regional Council, results in the severance of the northern tip of the park that includes Thornliebank Church and several cottages, including Newfield Cottage. At this time, the main entrance to the park is also moved from its historic location next to the Lodge (opposite Rowallan Road) to its current location. This opens up an opportunity for Eastwood District Council to market a site for development resulting in the Rouken Glen Garden Centre the next year.

Pond Open for Easter

The pond is to open to the public for Easter, the rowing boats and the pitch and putt will also be open.
(Mercury 20 April)

Nanette Davidson states 'I will never know how much influence my petition had on the authority's decision, but thankfully the amount of promotion and names on the petition raised the profile of the closure and the decision was taken by Eastwood District Council to take over the running of Rouken Glen and keep it as a park "due to local influence". Having now lived in Giffnock for 33 years, I have enjoyed many happy times with family, friends and visitors in Rouken Glen and I'm proud to say that I helped save the park so that many others continue to enjoy it too!'

Clubhouse to be Demolished

Eastwood decide that Deaconsbank Golf Course Clubhouse (formerly Deaconsbank Farm) should be demolished. It is in very poor condition and is deemed too dangerous to use, as part of the building has suffered a fire. The Council agree that once the Clubhouse is demolished, the area should be landscaped in a similar way to its surroundings. An offer by a builder to demolish the building is accepted on 28 August.
(Eastwood Council Minutes 29 June, 3, 13 and 28 August).

The Rouken Rally

24-27 May, Glasgow Scouting organise The Rouken Rally. The Rally is an adventure weekend for the Scouts and Venture Scouts Sections and is an open day for the Cub Section, parents, relatives and members of the public.

The whole park is divided up into activity sections including: rope making, orienteering, pancake making, trampolining, tug of war, circular football, fun fair, water activities with the police sub aqua team, and clay pigeon shooting.

The Scouts camp in the park all weekend and are awarded a badge for taking part in the adventure weekend.

John Brierley remembers The Rouken Rally, 'This was a long weekend camp, under canvas, for about 500 scouts from Eastwood District with some invited scouts from other areas in Scotland, and probably another 500 cubs and beavers who visited for the Saturday or the Sunday. I was the Camp Chief, but it was so busy that I don't have any real memories, apart from the fact that it was very successful.'

Gary Bainbridge of Clyde Scouts recalls a successful event with mixed weather. 'I have a particular vision of the opening ceremony when it was raining heavily. The grand finale was the release of balloons, which were contained under a tarpaulin. John Brierley gave the order "turn to face the balloons" at which point everyone turned to look at the dignitaries and guests standing next to the tarpaulin. After much merriment the tarpaulin was removed – and nothing happened! It was raining so hard that the balloons did not ascend until they were encouraged to do so!'

1985

Garden Centre Opens

Rouken Glen Garden Centre opens on 30 March. The Garden Centre Tearoom is located in the former Glasgow Corporation Tearoom of Birkenshaw stables.

Former Park Lodge house resident, Christine Goldsmith remembers the opening. 'It was initially just one big greenhouse. We got invited to the opening night because we lived in the park and to Christmas events. My husband, who worked for the Parks Department occasionally did a wee favour for the Garden Centre and I would get a big tray of plants as a thank you'.

The area where the Garden Centre now stands was known as the Horse Field. This was where the two Clydesdale horses grazed that were used for horse and cart rides in the park during the 1970s.

1986

Eastwood Butterfly Kingdom Opens

'Visitors will find hundreds of butterflies in extensive glasshousing, attractively landscaped in banks, streams and waterfalls crossed by little bridges to simulate the humid beauty of the tropical jungle. A wealth of exotic plants and flowers have been planted such as banana and orange trees, passion flowers, bamboo, stephanotis and bougainvillea. Some 600 butterflies inhabit the Butterfly Kingdom, representing 40 to 50 of the world's 2,000 or so species. While there will be some British species such as Small Tortoiseshell, Painted Lady and Red Admiral, the vast majority of butterflies and moths come from global tropical regions such as Malaysia, Brazil and Africa. Among the most spectacular are members of the Swallowtail family of very large butterflies which have wing spans from 4-7 inches and are vividly hued in black and yellow or black and red. The high humidity level required for the butterflies is provided by heating of 75-80o Fahrenheit and overhead sprinklers constantly rain on plants'.

In charge of the Butterfly Kingdom is Dr James Brock, an entomologist, and his assistant, Audrey Forrest, a botanist who gives talks to school parties.

A further area of interest in the Butterfly Kingdom is the insect house where, safely contained in glass tanks, are displayed scorpions, tarantula spiders, stick insects and leaf-eating ants *(Glasgow Herald 25 March)*

1987-88

Proposed Caravan Park

Advert in The Glasgow Herald on 26 August:
Although an access road was installed, the caravan park in the Meadow did not go ahead. Local resident Lena Ward believes it failed because of protests from residents in the Jenny Lind area of Deaconsbank.

Walled Garden Maintenance

Eastwood Council undertakes maintenance in the walled garden, repairing the arch, gates and fencing.

Above - *Entrance to Eastwood Butterfly Kingdom*
Map Flag 31

Above - *Walled Garden maintenance 1988*
Map Flag 04

Right - *Rouken Glen Meadow 2014. This part of Rouken Glen Park is also known by some visitors as the 'High Park'.*
Map Flag 11

Memories of Living Inside the Park

From 1988, Christine Goldsmith lived with her husband and family in one of the Rouken Glen Park lodge houses for 14 years.

Her daughters were 3 and 5 years old when they moved in. Christine's husband John worked for Eastwood District Council Park's Department in the park and in the workshop, now replaced by the Pro-Soccer centre.

'The lodge house was very cold; it had very thin insulation. There was only a coal fire inside. We managed to get central heating and double glazing put in. On a windy day the house moved because it was just timber. Otherwise the house was good, it was very dry, it was never damp. We had a lovely back garden and every year we had a garden party at the end of June and it never rained.

Despite living in the park, I didn't let the children use the playpark when they were very young. The hornbeam tree obscured the view so I couldn't keep an eye on them. When the park got really busy we retreated into the back garden because it was nice and private, especially in the height of summer when we looked out and saw a sea of people.

We liked the park when there was no-one else about and we had the park to ourselves, such as when everyone had gone home for dinner and the park was empty of visitors.

Christmas Day was nice when the park was very busy. Parents would come in with children and all their toys like bikes, scooters and toy prams.'

Christine's daughter Catherine loved it when the Irn Bru roadshow came with Radio Clyde to the park. 'They did a lot of sports. It came for quite a few years. I remember at the end of the event we all had lots of T-shirts, frisbees and a fridge stuffed full of Irn Bru! It was a big truck with an assault course and bales. There was a DJ on the truck and the music was going out live on the radio and we had to cheer at certain times.'

Catherine also recalls when it snowed. 'The whole park would be illuminated by the snow. We would get out of bed, put on our snowsuits and go out into the park. It was the only time we were allowed to stay up late. We would make a snowball that was so big, it would take three of us to push it. We loved to go sledging down the big hill in the Meadow as we would be the first there and we would get the best runs. We had to make sure we jumped off the sledge before hitting the burn at the bottom of the hill!'

Catherine believes The Pavilion Visitor Centre looks so much better now. It never used to look welcoming as it had big metal shutters. It was very dark inside and all that could be seen were the lights in the wee staff room at the back. It was the place for the parkies and you didn't mess with the parkies, especially as one was a former prison officer at Barlinnie!'

We liked the park when there was no-one else about and we had the park to ourselves

Christine Goldsmith remembers the tea room at Birkenshaw. 'It was a long building and there was a fountain inside. The tea room was painted red and grey inside. After the Garden Centre relocated their tea room to inside the Garden Centre, the Birkenshaw tea room closed and lay empty for a while before being converted into the Cathay Cuisine, a Cantonese Restaurant.'

The Chinese Restaurant had a table licence to sell alcohol with meals. This avoided Lord Rowallan's 'usual provision against the sale of liquor' by not selling alcohol direct to the public in a public bar. The Cantonese restaurant closed approximately 20 years later when it relocated out with the park.

1989

Garden Festival Gazebo

A gazebo from the 1988 Glasgow Garden Festival is transferred to Rouken Glen and stands on the former site of Thornliebank House.

Left - *Christine Goldsmith outside the Lodge House c1990*
Map Flag 36

Right - *Birkenshaw Cottage tea room c1986 before conversion into a Chinese restaurant*
Map Flag 35

Above - *One of the 1988 Glasgow Garden Festival Gazebos*
Map Flag 38

The 1990s

1992

Pavilion Refurbishment

The Pavilion receives a partial refurbishment to convert it from a picnic pavilion into a base for the Rouken Glen Park Rangers.

1992

Compulsory Competitive Tendering

Eastwood Council rejects the lowest bid in the last round of Compulsory Competitive Tendering for the ground maintenance of parks and open spaces owned by the council. A Code of Practice passed last year acknowledged there may be sound reason for declining the lowest bid. The Council claims the lowest bid failed to make proper provision to maintain Rouken Glen Park to a high standard. Emphasised was the failure to take account of the special requirements of Rouken Glen's walled garden and its security, as well as not taking account of the events that take place in the park every year. The contract was awarded to the council's Direct Services Organisation which had made the second lowest bid. The contract will take effect from 1 January 1993 for five years and three months. *(Extra 15 October)*

1993

The Butterfly Kingdom and Garden Centre

The Butterfly Kingdom attracts around 60,000 visitors a year. The visitors are mostly families and educational groups during the school term.

The Garden Centre is popular not only during the spring and summer months for the usual gardening activities but also prior to Christmas as it offers gifts and decorations for sale. *(Rouken Glen Park Development Plan July 1993)*

1995

Rouken Glen Photography Book

A book of photographs called 'Rouken Glen' by Neil Morris of Giffnock is gifted in a legacy to Eastwood Council. Neil loved Rouken Glen Park and was a keen photographer. He left money for the publication of his park photographs.

Eastwood Artsfest

Eastwood Artsfest is organised to celebrate 20 years of Eastwood District Council with events throughout the Council area. Rouken Glen Park played host to:

Lark In The Park – a five-hour family event featuring a Kite Extravaganza with 800 kites on one line, a mile high; street theatre, mime, sculpture, and a massive Eggopolis structure for youngsters to explore and make the day go with a swing.

Artsbeast – a week long opportunity to spot a skunk sculpture up a tree, discover canine creatures in different parts of the park or take a trip on a transparent boat to view sunken objects.

The Rite of Spring – featuring a family sculpture day with dance, music and street theatre. Fablevision's community theatre show involved a sunset procession of local children in costume transferring 'the staff of leadership' from King Winter to the Spring Goddess accompanied by music, lanterns and banners. The show culminates in a large bonfire and fireworks display. *(Herald 18, 25 April and 19 May)*

Christine Goldsmith remembers The Rite of Spring event. 'The kids learned a play about the rites of spring. My daughter Laura was a bee and she buzzed about and others dressed up as butterflies. Everybody came at night and walked through the Glen, a bit like Electric Glen but on a smaller scale. There were chainsaw sculpture carvings of owls hanging from the trees, a children's paper lantern parade and a firework display with a bonfire that went on to about midnight'.

Fire at Cleansing Shed

In May Eastwood Council's cleansing shed (situated in the area now used by Pro-soccer) is set on fire by vandals. John Goldsmith and Duncan Fordyce have to drive all the bin lorries out to save them. Staff lockers are damaged and personal items destroyed.

Boathouse Refurbishment Agreed

Eastwood Council agree to refurbish the boathouse into a cafe under the Tourism Partnership Programme. *(Eastwood Council Minutes 20 June)*

1996

Rouken Glen in Film

Rouken Glen is used for filming some scenes from Trainspotting. The park is substituted for The Meadows area of Edinburgh in the film. This is one of the iconic scenes in the film where Renton and Sick Boy discuss the career of Sean Connery, while preparing to shoot a skinhead's dog with an air rifle.

Duncan Fordyce recalls the filming. 'We knew nothing about the film so assumed the filming would be taking place along the railway line because the film was called Trainspotting. The filming was actually in the trees along the edge of the Glen and the dog was shot across to the opposite side of the Events Area. It was not like in the last 20 years when risk assessments have to be filled out!'

Other films and television programmes made in the park include Shallow Grave (1994), The Princess Stallion (1996), Still Game (2002–2007), Chewin' the Fat (1999–2005), Rab C Nesbitt (1988–2014) and Sea of Souls (2004–2007).

Duncan Fordyce also recalls a story about filming in the park for an episode of BBC TV's Rab C Nesbitt series during the 1990s. 'There was an old guy who worked in the park who was a chip short of a pack – Big John. The scene being recorded involved Rab C's pal Jamsie – the one with the ginger bottle. Old John used to clean up the park including the ginger bottles because at that time you got money back on the bottles. So John saw Jamsie walking in the park and went up to him and said "See when you are finished with that ginger bottle gonnae gie me it." Tony Roper (the actor playing the character of Jamsie) had to say "I cannae gie ye that ginger bottle mate" – to which John replied – "how can ye no gie me the ginger bottle?" – Tony Roper's response was "I cannae gie ye the ginger bottle because it's my prop."'

Council Changes

Another local government re-organisation with changes to council boundaries takes place. Glasgow District Council is renamed 'Glasgow City Council' and Eastwood District Council is replaced by the larger 'East Renfrewshire Council'. During the period 1975 to 1995 Glasgow and Eastwood were both District Councils within Strathclyde Regional Council. Rouken Glen Park remains out with the Glasgow Council administrative boundary.

The Princess Stallion

The Meadow is used to film scenes from the movie The Princess Stallion (1997). *(Extra 8 August)*

The European Pipe Band Championships

The European Pipe Band Championships is held in Rouken Glen Park with 135 UK pipe bands playing to crowds of over 20,000 people. There are competitions for the pipes, drums and highland dancers as well as entertainment for all the family including clowns and magicians. The free event is organised by East Renfrewshire Council and the Royal Scottish Pipe Band Association. *(Extra 12 September)*

The previous year, Williamwood Pipe Band Major Andy Melvin attended a Royal Scottish Pipe Band Association (RSPBA) meeting where a discussion took place regarding possible venues to host the European Pipe Band Championships in 1996. 'I suggested Rouken Glen Park and unaware that the RSPBA was taking forward my suggestion, I accepted an invitation from East Renfrewshire Council to travel to their twin town, Albertslund in Copenhagen, Denmark as part of a town twinning event. The visit was on the same weekend as the European Pipe Band Championships, so unfortunately Williamwood Pipe Band was unable to take part.'

1997

Sports Centre Disputes

Lord Rowallan, great-grandson of Archibald Cameron Corbett who gifted Rouken Glen Park to the citizens of Glasgow, backs campaigners against a proposal to expand Deaconsbank Golf Course into the Meadow of Rouken Glen Park. Sports Management (Scotland) Ltd, who operate Deaconsbank Golf Course, want to build an indoor tennis and leisure centre for David Lloyd Leisure on the club's driving range which will be moved onto the fairway, necessitating the expansion of the golf course into the Meadow. A petition against the proposal has been signed by 7,500 people and, as well as Lord Rowallan, objectors include Glasgow Council. Parklands Country Club in Newton Mearns – a similar leisure development to the one proposed for Rouken Glen and already based in East Renfrewshire, is considering legal action if the proposal goes ahead. They say that when Parklands opened in 1989, Eastwood Council agreed that it would not enter into an agreement with other similar developments on council owned land for 20 years. *(Herald 29 October)*

Butterfly Kingdom Closes

Eastwood Butterfly Kingdom closes in 1997 when it became no longer viable.

Left - *The European Pipe Band Championships 1996*

Right - *The dry stane dyke on the Glen path near the waterfall in Rouken Glen Map Flag 19*

1998

Highland Games

Rouken Glen hosts Highland Games on Sunday 7 June. The event attracts around 6,000 people who enjoy Highland dancers and the strong man competition. For children there are mini highland games, face painting and a puppet show, among other attractions. *(Extra 11 June)*

David Lloyd Leisure Planning

Sports Management (Scotland) Ltd and David Lloyd Leisure submit a new planning application for an indoor tennis and leisure centre following the public outcry to their previous application. The proposal is to build the centre on the site of the existing Deaconsbank Golf Course Clubhouse and driving range, outwith the area of Rouken Glen which was gifted by Archibald Cameron Corbett in 1906. *(Extra 19 November)*

East Renfrewshire Council grants planning permission for the development in 1999. *(Extra 30 September)*

1999

Sustrans Scotland

In April a dry stane dyke artwork is built in the Glen by Sustrans Scotland (who are responsible for expanding the National Cycle Network - providing stimulating, memorable environments through which walkers and cyclists can travel safely). Sustrans worked with artist David F Wilson to create a new rampway allowing easier access to lower areas of the Glen for walkers and cyclists. Built on site over a six week period using locally sourced whinstone, the work created an organic natural look that sits easily within its surroundings. Built within the walls are a series of nooks and alcoves that suggest the mystery of the woods, perhaps little spaces where offerings to spirits who live there could be left.

21st Century
in the park

With a young and vibrant population surrounding the park, the focus is on improving facilities for the next generation so that the park can enjoy another successful hundred years.

Discover what's happened so far in the 21st Century

*One of the many events
held in the park
Map Flag 03*

2003

K7X

K7X (now Pro-Soccer) opens offering 5 and 7 a-side football on all-weather pitches on the site of the former Eastwood Council Recycling Centre and Glasgow Corporation garage, beside Rouken Glen Garden Centre.

2005

Skate Park Installed

A skate park is installed in Rouken Glen at a cost of £120,000.

Below - *The skate park in use*
Map Flag 05

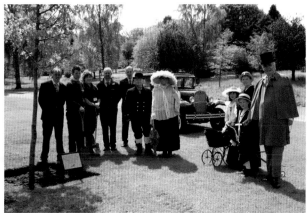

2006

Historic Scotland

31 March: Rouken Glen Park is recorded by Historic Scotland in its inventory of gardens and designed landscapes. The park is complimented for its value as a work of art; some historical value; horticultural, arboricultural, silvicultural value with bedding displays in the walled garden and specimen parkland trees; scenic value; archaeological value for its cup and ring marked rocks and outstanding nature conservation value for its Site of Special Scientific Interest.

The Centenary of the opening of the park

Three granite standing stones are erected to mark the park's centenary and a time capsule containing local papers, local history DVDs, coins, stamps and a copy of a Harry Potter book are buried to provide future generations with an insight into what life was like in 2006.

2009

Veterinary Surgery Opens

September - Rouken Glen Veterinary Surgery opens in the refurbished East Lodge.

Top Left - Centenary standing stone and time capsule
Map Flag 20

Above - Comparison of the clothes and items young people use in the park

Top Right - A young oak tree is planted in Rouken Glen Park on 25 May 2006 to commemorate, almost 100 years to the day, when the park was gifted to the community by Archibald Cameron-Corbett MP, later Lord Rowallan.

2012-16
The Heritage Lottery Fund Parks for People Project

By early 2000, Rouken Glen Park – although a popular and well-loved park, is beginning to show its age after a century of public use. In recognition of this East Renfrewshire Council develops a plan of restoration and modernisation.

With 'in principle' support from the Heritage Lottery Fund (including an initial funding award of £123,000), project development work culminates in a full bid to the Heritage Lottery Fund (HLF) Parks For People programme seeking £2.15 million to match the £1 million contribution from East Renfrewshire Council.

In July 2012 HLF announces the application has been successful. This means four years of works to restore park features will go ahead alongside the delivery of a range of events, activities, volunteering and learning opportunities.

Most of the funding will be spent on key physical projects:

– Refurbishment of the Pavilion and installation of a new park heritage exhibition
– Restoration of the walled garden
– Restoration and extension of the Glen Walk and rebuilding of two bridges
– New path lighting, installation of electrical power cabinets and park access improvements
– New park signage throughout
– Planting and other improvements to the pond
– Installation of a new play park, outdoor gym equipment and other outdoor play facilities
– Investigation and clearance of the geological Site of Special Scientific Interest
– Archaeological surveys and investigations and the restoration of the dovecot.

Left - Path lighting installed on the path between the two car parks in the park

Top - Electrical power cabinet installed in the park's Events Area
Map Flag 03

Middle - One of 11 pieces of Outdoor Gym equipment installed in 2014 on a circuit in the park

Bottom - Main park entrance after improvements 2015
Map Flag 08

Heritage Lottery Funded Improvements in Rouken Glen Park

Images on opposite page

Top Left – *Rouken Glen Park's Conservation Volunteers, cutting down bamboo (May 2013)*

Top Right – *Family activity, Trees a Crowd (April 13)*

Middle Left – *Evening talk, Landscape photography (December 2014)*

Middle Right – *Crookfur Primary School, Plant identification (June 13)*

Bottom Left – *Remembering the Rookie, Reminiscence Event with the Kirkton Service and Our Lady of the Missions Primary (April 2015)*

Bottom Right – *Woodfarm High School, Removing Tree Guards (November 2014)*

The improvements through the HLF project make the park more accessible, more enjoyable and more heritage-friendly. Visitor numbers to the park increase greatly as does recognition of the park's value as a public greenspace.

As important as the physical improvements to the park is the need to encourage and support greater community involvement in the park.

The Friends of Rouken Glen are established in 2009 to work with East Renfrewshire Council to develop park projects, assist with park activities and promote the park to a wider audience. FORG continues to undertake this role until 2014 when the group disbands.

The HLF project enabled two activity staff to be employed to develop and lead volunteering projects, organise events and activities, and engage with the public to help extend people's knowledge and enjoyment of Rouken Glen Park.

Another crucial element of the project to to ensure that the park's management and maintenance are heritage sensitive to ensure that the improvements made under the HLF project are sustained into the future.

Above – *the pond after improvements 2016 – the two larger islands have been cleared of rhododendron; the water has been treated to reduce the weed and algae growth, aquatic planting has been introduced to filter phosphates from the water and to enhance the aesthetics of the pond and two platforms have been built to give better access for pond dipping education activities and for the Model Steamer Club to launch their boats.*
Map Flag 02

Some of the many activities overseen by Rouken Glen Park's Activities Staff.

Since 2012 Rouken Glen Park has had a full-time Activity Ranger based in the Pavilion Visitor Centre to oversee volunteering and education activities in the park.

Highlights of Rouken Glen Park
The Pavilion Visitor Centre

Very little is recorded about the former Picnic Pavilion built in 1910. It was used as an army canteen during 1941-44 and is now Rouken Glen Park's Visitor Centre and home to the park ranger service.

Above - The Pavilion after refurbishment in 2014

Top Left - The Pavilion prior to refurbishment in 2012 Map Flag 33

Top Right - The 'Story of Rouken Glen' Exhibition opened in 2014 in the refurbished Pavilion Visitor Centre

Bottom Left - The interior of the Pavilion prior to refurbishment

Bottom Middle - The new meeting space created after refurbishment

Bottom Right - The bespoke reception desk in the Pavilion Visitor Centre, designed by Paul Hodgkiss Designs from fallen timber from Rouken Glen

When the refurbishment of the Pavilion started in 2013 it was quickly realised that the condition of the building was much worse than thought. Extensive rot was found along the rear section of the building – extending into the main hall. It was also found that the front of the property was 'leaning out' by several centimetres.

At this point consideration was given to its demolition and replacement with a modern building however, after consultation with the Friends of Rouken Glen, it was clear that the preference was to keep the historic structure. The greater than anticipated refurbishment has however resulted in a bright, warm, accessible and adaptable space that retains many of the architectural features so beloved of park visitors.

2013

Events in the Park

Over the years Rouken Glen Park has played host to a large number of community events attracting large numbers of visitors to the park.

The size of the park lends itself to a variety of activities with many nooks and crannies being utilised by local groups and organisations to promote their own activities.

Notable events include Highland Games featuring many famous strong men and women from across Scotland. Among the popular attractions are the traditional heavy events, with professional athletes competing for the honours. These include the caber toss, hammer throw and shot putt, and the international women's highland challenge, with Highland events and strength challenges. Also featured is the ever-popular women's welly-throwing contest, children's entertainment and activities, farmers' market, historical re-enactment, food stalls and an arts and crafts fair.

Rouken Glen is host to its first Festival of Colour, celebrating the Hindu Holi ('colour') Festival. The highlight is the 'colour play' where people 'adorn' each other with eco-friendly coloured powder to welcome in the new season. The event is organised by Maryhill Integration Network who were unable to find an accommodating park in Glasgow.

The fifth FeastRen weekend food festival focusing on local food and drink is held in Rouken Glen.

Other events include Community Fun days organised by local group Cascade, Running Festivals organised by Giffnock Athletic Club and Tartan day celebrating Scotland and its links to the Scottish diaspora.

Top - *Highland Games, April 2013*
Middle - *Holi Festival of Colour, 30 July 2016*

Bottom - *FeastRen - East Renfrewshire Food Festival, 21 and 22 September 2013*

2014

Young Enterprise Scotland Academy

28 March is the official opening of Young Enterprise Scotland Academy at Rouken Glen Park. £400,000 has been invested in the Academy and over 500 young people have participated in a wide variety of programmes since last year. The Academy aims to address gaps in training provision to help young people into sustainable employment.

Glasgow 2014 Commonwealth Games Queen's Baton Relay

On 16 July the Glasgow 2014 Commonwealth Games Queen's Baton Relay runs through the park as part of its visit to East Renfrewshire and a large number of people participate in a variety of sports and other activities offered throughout the day linked to the Games.

Electric Glen

During February 2013, 2014 and 2016, the Electric Glen festival transforms Rouken Glen Park into a multi-coloured wonderland for several nights. The temporary lighting installation illuminates features in the Glen and around the boating pond – transporting visitors to a magical world of light and sound, and allowing visitors to experience the park in a night time setting. Over the three years Electric Glen attracts over 66,000 visitors.

Top - *Official opening of Young Enterprise Scotland Academy in Rouken Glen Park*

Middle - *The Queen's Baton Relay passes in front of the Pavilion Visitor Centre in Rouken Glen Park*
Map Flag 33

Bottom - *The islands and boating pond illuminated in February 2014.*
Map Flag 02

2012 - 2016

Armed Forces Day

Armed Forces Day takes place in Rouken Glen Park. This is an annual, national celebration to give people the opportunity to show their support for the men and women who make up the Armed Forces community – from serving troops to service families, and from veterans to cadets.

2015

David Lloyd Plans Approved

David Lloyd Leisure submits a revised planning application reducing the size of their indoor tennis and leisure centre on the site of the former Deaconsbank Golf Clubhouse and driving range. East Renfrewshire Council approves the plans and building work commences thereafter.

Left – *Armed Forces Day June 2015*

Right – *Park staff and Councillor Vincent Waters, Environment Convenor, with the Green Flag.*

Fifth Green Flag

Rouken Glen Park is awarded its fifth Green Flag, a sign to visitors that the park is well-maintained and well-managed, with excellent facilities.

Rouken Glen Park is one of 65 parks and green spaces awarded the honour in Scotland.

4-Star Award

May 2016, Visit Scotland gives Rouken Glen Park a 4-star award for the second year in a row.

2016

Celebration Day

Towards the end of the HLF project, 'Rouken Glen Celebration Day' takes place on 30th July to showcase the achievements of the last four years. Storytelling, dramas, eco-zone activities, guided walks, fairground rides and music take place alongside the ever-popular Festival of Colour. Crowds of nearly 7000 come along to celebrate the improvements that have taken place and to join in the fun.

2016 and Beyond

Parks Manager Donnie McManus says, 'With the Heritage Lottery Project now complete East Renfrewshire Council will continue to build on all the excellent work that has taken place throughout the project. The Council will continue to develop the park, embrace new ideas, source new funding and work with the many volunteer and diverse groups who have contributed to the project.

Visitor numbers reached nearly one million in 2015 – mainly due to the many positive changes in the park that the Heritage Lottery Fund award, with Council support, was able to bring. The 2015 Park Visitor Survey indicated an incredible 99% satisfaction with the park.'

The challenge for the Council will be to continue this good work and ensure that the park will be with us for the next one hundred years.'

Bibliography

A list of the main sources consulted; a fully sourced version of the historical parts of this publication is available at Giffnock Community Library.

Books

Adams, J., Letters from the Front 1914-1919 http://johnadams.org.uk/letters/
Anon., Crum's Land – A History of Thornliebank (East Renfrewshire Council 1988).
Anon., Sandstone to Suburbia – A History of Giffnock (East Renfrewshire Council 1988).
Blair, A., Old Giffnock, (Stenlake 2003).
Brotchie, R.W. & Grieves, R.L., Paisley's Trams and Buses 1880s to 1920s.
Corporation of Glasgow, Municipal Glasgow, its evolution and enterprises, (R Gibson & Sons, Glasgow, 1914).
Crosbie, A., Liddell, M. and Young, P. Thornliebank Time Travellers, Childhood Memories, (Grimalkin Press, Glasgow, 2004).
Devine, M., Old Thornliebank, (Stenlake 2005).
Fraser, W., Memorials of the Montgomeries, Earls of Eglinton (1859).
Glasgow Corporation Minutes, The Mitchell Library, Glasgow.
Journal of Film Preservation, Glasgow: Scottish Film Archive, Anonymous. 24.51 (Nov 1995): 30-33, ProQuest LLC
Macintosh, T., Rouken Glen Illustrated (J Cosser, Glasgow, 1915).
Mapping the Practice and Profession of Sculpture in Britain & Ireland 1851-1951 http://sculpture.gla.ac.uk/view/object.php?id=msib7_1205419153
Mertz, Caroline., 2016, Why Not a Scots Hollywood? Fiction Film Production in Scotland 1911-1928. PhD thesis, University of Edinburgh
Millar, A.H., The Castles and Mansions of Renfrewshire and Buteshire (T & R Annan & Sons, Glasgow, 1889).
Morris, N., Rouken Glen (J Thomson, Glasgow, 1995).
Nisbet, S., 'The Hidden History of Rouken Glen' and 'Mearns Bleachfields & Printfields' Mearns History Group website.
Nisbet, S., The Rise of the Cotton Factory in 18th Century Renfrewshire (Archaeopress 2008).
Taylor, Charles, Rouken Glen & Its Neighbourhood by (F W Wilson, Glasgow, 1907).
Tobias, M., The Barony of Eastwood (held at Giffnock Heritage Centre).
University of Glasgow Archive Services, Papers of Sir Archibald Cameron Corbett, 1856-1933, 1st Baron of Rowallan.
Welsh, T.C., Eastwood District, History and Heritage (1989).
Whitton, J., Public Parks of Glasgow (Journal of the Royal Horticultural Society, Vol XLV, Part I, 1919).

Newspapers

The Scotsman, The (Glasgow) Herald, The (Glasgow South and Eastwood) Extra, The Mercury (later The Mercury and Eastwood Advertiser), The Scotsman, The Daily Record and Mail, The Edinburgh Evening News, The Glasgow Evening Telegraph, The Bulletin, The Courier [Dundee], The Daily Record (and Mail), The Aberdeen Press and Journal, The Times, The Sunday Post, The Falkirk Herald, The South Side News and Glasgow Advertiser (most of these newspapers can be searched on line to find Rouken Glen news).

Additional information from Illustrated Magazine.

Libraries and Archives

British Library Board, National Library of Scotland for: Glasgow Post Office & Renfrewshire Directories, Maps, The Scotsman digital archive, Eglinton Plans (RHP3/156 - 173). Giffnock Heritage Centre, Giffnock Library, Glasgow City Archives for: Crum Papers (TD 1073/15/1), Abridged Sasines for Renfrewshire (T-SA7/1/2).

Reminiscences by John Adams, James Bone, John Brierley, Jack Cook, Nanette Davidson, May Fabiani, Duncan Fordyce, Catherine Goldsmith, Christine Goldsmith, May Leckie, Dorothy McBride, Roderick McDougall, Ross McKemmie, Andy Melvin, Rochelle Moore, Hugh Nelson, Alistair and Catherine Raeburn, Grace Smith, George Thomson, Lena and Robert Ward. Reminiscences by William Brown and Ann Crosbie first published in Thornliebank Time Travellers Childhood Memories.

Additional contributions from Donnie McManus, Sharon McMurtrie and Malcolm Wright of East Renfrewshire Council, Gary Bainbridge of Clyde Scouts, John West of East Renfrewshire Designed Landscapes and Gardens Group, David F Wilson, Stuart Nisbet and Liz Rodger.

Photographs from Archaeology Scotland, D C Thomson & Co Ltd, Earl of Eglinton & Winton, East Renfrewshire Council Communications, East Renfrewshire Library and Information Services, Johnston Publishing Ltd, Scotsman Publications Ltd, Trinity Mirror Publishing Ltd, Anna Blair, Gary Bainbridge, John Cunningham, Maud Devine, Gibson Digital, David Gillon, Christine Goldsmith, Peter Johnson, Elaine Livingstone Photography, Sharon McMurtrie, Andy Melvin, Neil Morris, Odhams Press Ltd, Stuart Nisbet, Liz Rodger, Harry Rutherford, Norman Schulman, David F Wilson.